LLEWELLYN'S

Little Book of

MEDITATION

© Linda Townsend

David Pond is an astrologer, author, speaker, and international workshop leader. He is the author of six previous books on metaphysical topics, including *Chakras for Beginners*, *Astrology and Relationships*, and *Western Seeker, Eastern Paths*. David can be found online at his website: DavidPond.com.

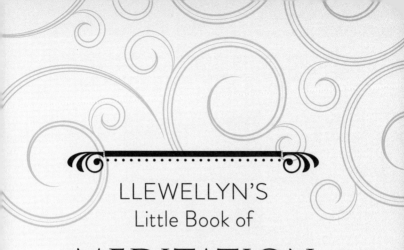

LLEWELLYN'S
Little Book of

MEDITATION

DAVID POND

LLEWELLYN PUBLICATIONS
WOODBURY, MINNESOTA

FIRST EDITION
First Printing, 2018

Based on book design by Rebecca Zins
Cover cartouche by Freepik
Cover design by Lisa Novak
Interior illustrations on page 126 by the Llewellyn Art Department,
on page 133 by Mary Ann Zapalac

Llewellyn Publications is a registered trademark of Llewellyn Worldwide Ltd.

Library of Congress Cataloging-in-Publication Data is pending.

ISBN 978-0-7387-5418-5

Llewellyn Publications
A Division of Llewellyn Worldwide Ltd.
2143 Wooddale Drive
Woodbury, MN 55125-2989
www.llewellyn.com

Printed in China

Dedication

To all of the budding Buddhas who seek to bring more
peace into their lives and the world.

Acknowledgments

The process of bringing the original idea for a book to its ultimate publication always amazes me. I start off with such inspiration and then realize my original ideas first written down are the proverbial diamond in the rough, needing a great deal of crafting, refining, and polishing to make the material readable for others. As part of the process I have grown to value and even depend on feedback from those who have graciously been willing to read drafts along the way. I will be forever grateful to my wife, Laurie, for taking on the yeoman's task of editing the first drafts. Her patience with helping me forge these into a coherent form always amazes me.

I would first like to thank Angela Wix, acquisitions editor at Llewellyn Publications, for suggesting that I write a book on meditation, and then for her valuable insights and suggestions along the way to bringing this to its final form.

I would like to acknowledge the following friends and family members for reading the manuscript and offering their valuable personal insights: Lynn Mitchell, Forest Pond, Geri Herbert, Amy Stolzenbach, Heather Islander,

Michele McIntyre, Kim Myhre, Julie Myhre, Rick Salsbery, Skylar Pond, and Cheryl Welch. Each of you will see your suggestions incorporated into the final draft, and I am so thankful you were willing to share your insights for improving the book.

And finally a special acknowledgment to my soul-buddy Andria Friesen for her willingness to share her attentive eye with me, line by line, as we went through the manuscript together. As owner of the Friesen Art Gallery in Ketchum, Idaho, she has a trained eye for the aesthetics in all she does and gently offered her many insights for improving the presentation of the material.

I would also like to express my gratitude for the lineage of teachers who have kept the teachings of meditation alive throughout history, as well as modern teachers who graciously share their teachings and wisdom of this ancient practice in the world today.

Contents

∽

Exercises

Exercises for Children

Do you often wish that you could just stop your thoughts and experience a little peace of mind? Learning to meditate can do just that for you. If you have ever had doubts about your ability to be successful at meditation, this book will likely change your mind. And by beginning a meditation practice, you will change your mind—literally. As you will learn, meditation is not simply sitting and doing nothing; it is actively training your mind to stay focused on the object of your meditation, and then, as your mind quiets, to open to expanded awareness. Although the experience of one session is enjoyable and beneficial in and of itself, if you develop a daily practice, even after a few weeks you will experience noticeable transformations in your life, including an increased ability to concentrate, diminished stress and anxiety, greater patience, and diminished restlessness, to name just a few of the benefits. You will also notice greater clarity and discernment in making choices throughout the day that comes from tapping into your inner knowing and wisdom beyond your mind.

This book will give you insights and the tools you need to calm your busy mind and open to another dimension of your being: calm and spacious awareness. Meditation cultivates a domain of your consciousness that is always available, but that we are normally unaware of. Through this book we will explore what meditation is and isn't, the origins of meditation, and various styles of meditation, so that you will be able to find the style and technique that works best for you to gain the wonderful benefits that come from incorporating meditation into your life.

A Little Bit about Me

I am a professional astrologer and metaphysician, and have been for over thirty-five years. I have also been a yoga and meditation teacher and, with my wife, Laurie, have led many groups to sacred sites around the world for a week of exploring, metaphysical studies, yoga, and meditation. My own experiences with transcendent states started very early in life and in a most unfriendly way, with a recurring energy nightmare that would wake me up in a state of panic throughout my youth.

I call it an "energy" nightmare because there were never any images or a story line, as with other dreams—only a swirling vortex of energy that scared the bejesus out of me! It could happen several nights a week: Shortly after falling off to sleep, I would see this swirling vortex of energy above me and feel myself getting pulled into it. As soon as I would feel a surge of energy from the vortex, I could feel it being more powerful than anything I could control, and a terrible and all too familiar feeling of panic would come over me. This would wake me up with a shock, and I would find myself sitting up in a cold sweat, gasping for breath. After sitting there stunned for a while,

I would eventually go back to sleep, and fortunately these energy dreams never occurred twice in the same night.

This went on until I was fourteen, when a totally unique encounter I had with this energy vortex changed everything. On this particular night, I had fallen asleep listening to a Seattle University basketball game, my favorite local team, and when the vortex appeared, instead of pulling back in fear, I surrendered to the energy. As I became engulfed in the power, I found myself hovering above the game I had been listening to when I fell asleep, and I was able to send the power to the Seattle players. It was exhilarating! Basketball players who can jump over their opponents have a decided advantage, and my supercharged Seattle players could do just that and more, easily winning, to my delight.

From that night on, these still frequent dreams with the energy vortex became welcome encounters that I grew to treasure. I loved the sense of limitless possibilities they gave me—far better than the previous sense of panic, which never returned. I grew to like these special dreams so much that I became curious as to whether I could invoke the same feeling in the daytime.

Experimenting, I somehow found a way of working with my imagination that would invoke the same experience as my energy dreams. I would close my eyes and imagine a cartoon image of a rocket ship, like something I might have seen in a Woody Woodpecker cartoon. I would then see myself standing on the ground next to the rocket, looking at another "me" who was sitting in the rocket and simultaneously looking at the me on the ground.

I would then feel the rocket begin to take off and maintain watching myself both in the rising rocket and on the ground—both me's watching each other. I could feel the sensation of rising up as the two me's separated from each other, and before long I could feel the familiar spaciousness of my dream state. I developed a measure for knowing if I had gotten to that state or not: if I couldn't tell if it was an inch or a mile between my lips, I knew I was there.

This practice became a secret treasure that I kept to myself throughout high school and that I would take refuge in during stolen moments when it looked like I was taking a nap. I had never heard anyone talk about such experiences, so I kept it private. In my early college years I had become interested in Eastern mysticism and was reading *Zen Flesh, Zen Bones,* a book of Zen parables by Paul Reps. After the parables, there is a section called "The Gateless

Gate" with a number of Zen meditation exercises, and I decided to try a few. Following the instructions, I focused on my posture and my breath and practiced watching my thoughts. To my amazement, within a few minutes I found myself experiencing the same expansive awareness and feeling of separation from my body that I did in my secret place!

This experience blew my mind. I had thought my inner journeys were unique to me, so I was amazed to discover that this state is well known in other traditions, complete with training available to refine this skill. I felt like the proverbial kid in a candy store and have been studying and experimenting with meditation ever since.

I haven't always been regular with my meditation practice, but I have learned that when I am out of sorts for too long, overly impatient with others, and easily agitated, it is a clear sign that I need to get back to meditating regularly. And when I do, the spaciousness I experience in meditation comes back into my life again. There is more space in me to allow others to be as they are, more space in me to allow life to unfold at its pace.

About Meditation and This Book

Everyone can learn to meditate. We will start right at the beginning with what meditation is, to give those new to it a strong foundation to start their inner exploration. There will be various exercises and practices to engage in throughout the book to give you the actual experience of what is being described. Many different styles and applications of meditation will be explored, and with just a little training, your skill at achieving a calm mind to explore your inner world will improve.

First off, in learning to observe your mind, you will become more familiar with your inner terrain and begin to see the patterns of your mind that distract your inner calm. Knowing your way around your inner world lets you know when you are off-track and what adjustments you need to make to stay in a state of calm awareness. Over time, these adjustments you make to retrain your mind produce long-term structural changes in your brain and its circuitry.

There have been many advances in our understanding of the brain with recent discoveries in neuroscience. In the early 1980s when I was pursuing a master of science degree in experimental metaphysics, the science for understanding the intuitive arts was still rather sketchy. Most of the studies at that time were based on the statistical probability of accurately predicting events, rather than what was actually occurring in the brain.

Up until recently, it was commonly believed that the brain quits growing and evolving by early adulthood. Advances in modern technology's ability to map and measure what is actually going on in the brain have revealed that the brain possesses the capacity to reorganize neural networks, create new connections, and even create new neurons throughout life. This is popularly called the brain's *plasticity*—its ability to grow, adapt, and even change in shape and size.

Furthermore, it was previously believed that consciousness was to be found in the neural circuitry of the brain. With the practice of meditation, you will discover that your consciousness is larger than your mind. The emerging new understanding is that your brain is secondary to your consciousness. Your consciousness is larger than your brain and can choose how it operates. As you develop in consciousness, you begin to see your brain as presenting possibilities that you can choose to act on or not. The "you" that can make choices that your mind presents as options is the "you" that you get in touch with in meditation.

You are not limited by the hardwiring of your brain. By practicing meditation regularly, you create new neural networks in your brain, making it easier and easier to sustain a state of calm awareness within while engaging in life more openly.

The way to measure your progress with your meditation practice is by gauging your ability to stay in a state of open awareness throughout the day, the openness you develop for other people and life itself, and your growing patience with others and yourself. These are valuable measures. In some of your meditations you may receive incredible flashes of insight or magical visions, which are welcome visitors that come of their own accord. More often, meditation is training yourself to experience a calm mind and actually changing the way your brain works. We now know that "firing is wiring" in the neural networks of the brain: neurons that fire together form neural networks that become ingrained as habitual responses. It is also true that when neurons no longer fire together, their network dissolves, liberating you from ingrained reactionary patterns. By training yourself to stay anchored in your peaceful, open awareness, this habit

One of the benefits that
you will grow to appreciate is
how your meditation practice
can have a centering effect
on those you interact with,
even if they are not meditators.

becomes ingrained in the neural networks of your brain and begins to be the norm.

One of the benefits that you will grow to appreciate is how your meditation practice can have a centering effect on those you interact with, even if they are not meditators. There was a time when my sons were in school that I grew to realize this. My wife and I are blessed with great children who mostly knew how to stay out of trouble while growing up. However, there were patches of time when chaos and trouble seemed to abound—difficulties with teachers, scuffles, car mishaps, and the like. At that time in my life I was a periodic meditator, and it was during one of those tough spots for the family that I realized these times of difficulty seemed to coincide with times when I had drifted away from my meditation practice. Realizing there was no center in the family chaos, I returned to my practice of centering myself with meditation.

It wasn't as if I pictured myself sending balanced, centered energy to my family; I simply returned to my own work of calming my mind and sitting in peaceful awareness, knowing my family was already in my heart and energetically connected to me. Returning to my meditation practice always seemed to help bring the family back into harmony.

Understanding Resistance to Meditation

Why is it that many people believe they are not able to meditate? Everyone can learn to meditate and everyone can benefit from the practice. Let's examine some of the reasons people give for not taking up meditation.

"I Can't Find the Time to Meditate"

This is the most common reason given by those who are interested in starting a meditation practice but keep putting it off. Where is there time to sit and do nothing when there isn't enough time already to get everything done that needs to be done? In our modern hurry, hurry, rush, rush world, it can seem impossible to take time away from all of the busyness to stop and meditate. But consider how much time in the day is wasted in idle distractions and worrying about the past or future rather than effectively focusing on the situation at hand. How much time is spent in escapist activities or simply getting lost in social media as a way of escaping the here and now?

There is a paradox that meditators discover: time spent in inner practice is easily regained throughout the day. Your concentration and focus improve, allowing you to get more done in less time with improved quality by harvesting all of the time that is normally lost from your mind distracting you from the immediate task at hand. With a little bit of training, the mind is easily called back from its wanderings to stay present with focused attention.

Outside of the time you set aside for sitting meditation practices, time for meditation can be found at traffic lights, during stalled traffic, or in endlessly slow-moving lines when you are not going anywhere anyway. Times like these are perfect for a few breathing and centering exercises, training your mind to move out of a normally agitating experience and into peaceful, calm awareness.

"My Mind Won't Stop Thinking When I Try to Meditate"

This most common problem is common because it is normal. The experience of having your mind distract you from your attempts to meditate with a constant flow of seemingly important thoughts is a reality everyone deals with and must be understood for it not to be an obstacle. Many people never get out of their minds and believe they are whatever their thoughts tell them about themselves, for good or bad. Although you cannot stop your mind from thinking thoughts, you can train yourself not to follow them and their fleeting opinions. As you sit with your practice of quieting your mind, know that thoughts *will* come, but set your attention to return to the object of your meditation, like following your breath or repeating your mantra.

As you continue with the practice of noticing the voices in your head but not paying attention to them, they eventually quiet—somewhat. You begin to identify with the spiritual essence of your unchanging awareness as your true self and realize that all of the passing thoughts are just that—passing thoughts that can't even be held on to—nothing substantial to thoughts at all.

Imagine that your mind is going to be throwing sticks in front of you as you attempt to meditate. Do you want to be like a young dog chasing after every moving stick, or do you want to train yourself to be like a lion, maintaining your composure while observing the fleeting sticks and being selective about what you want to pursue? Another useful image is to consider yourself to be the flight controller in your mind. Your mind has all of these incoming and outgoing flights of thought, but you, as the controller, do not have to get on board or follow any of this traffic. If something critical presents itself, you can jump into action. Otherwise, you are just observing the coming in and going out of all the flights.

Meditation is training yourself not to listen to all the yammering voices in your head so that you can hear the still, quiet voice of your Higher Self. It does take a bit of courage and curiosity to let go of the mind's tendency to seek to figure everything out, and to trust that life will be just fine without your mind directing it.

"Meditation Seems Boring"

The fact that meditation can seem boring is another common reason people don't take up the practice. Compared to the mind's fascinations, training yourself to sit with your breath and focus your attention on the here and now can seem dull. Allow this to be. Meditating without a goal of achieving any special state of consciousness can be very helpful. Goals for why to take up a meditation practice (such as to experience peace of mind, relieve stress and anxiety, develop greater patience, or other valuable motivations) are helpful in the background, but it is best to let go of those goals while actually in your practice. Take a "nothing special here" approach and sit with the feeling of this being boring—just the truth of you and your thoughts in the present moment.

Boredom sets in when the mind anticipates something more exciting than sitting in silence and it begins to scan for possible future peak experiences. While your mind is anticipating some alluring, tantalizing next thing, it misses so much of the here and now between peak events. With a little practice, you begin to find fulfillment in simply sitting and no longer looking for the next peak—you start enjoying the plains and valleys as well. This has tremendous benefit throughout the day, giving you much greater patience with life as it is and increasing your ability to enjoy life's simple pleasures along the way between peak experiences.

෨

There is not just one type of meditation. There are many schools of thought on this inner practice, with many various techniques being taught. They all share the common basis of quieting the mind with breath and concentration, leading to a peace of mind unknown without training. Throughout this book you will have opportunities to experience firsthand various meditation techniques and styles so that you may find a practice that is most comfortable for you to experience the tremendous benefits this inner science affords—so let's begin!

Chapter One

WHAT IS MEDITATION?

Why would a person want to learn to meditate? First of all, meditation calms your busy mind, restoring a sense of peace and well-being within you. Meditation is training your mind to move away from distracting and destructive patterns toward peaceful attention to the immediate moment. Our everyday mind, often called the "monkey mind," jumps all over the place—dwelling on the past, anticipating the future, and manifesting anxiety ceaselessly. Meditation is the practice of training your mind to stay focused on the object of your concentration with single-minded attention. In doing so, you become aware of another level of your being that is peacefully observing all of your mental activity. Awakening to awareness is the essence of meditation. With the practice of taming your restless body and mind, you become more familiar with the spacious awareness that arises and its qualities of unchanging tranquility, calmness, and peace.

Changes in Your Brain from Meditation

Training yourself to return to your peaceful awareness has obvious immediate benefits, but meditating over time actually changes your brain's neural circuitry. Your brain is not hardwired to always and only respond in certain ways. Patterns are formed in the brain through the principle of "firing is wiring"; neurons that repeatedly fire together will create a neural network, like an automatic pathway. When you retrain your mind not to fire off in a reactionary mode, new neurological networks are created. *It is not that you just get better at dealing with difficult thoughts and emotions when they arise—many quit arising!*

Joe Dispenza, in his book *Evolve Your Brain*, cites many studies that show actual significant changes in the brain occurring for those who practice meditation—enhancing learning, memory, problem solving, and centers that regulate emotions in the brain. The brain's center for managing stress also grows, diminishing stress-related problems.

Just as important as the increase in size and function of helpful centers within the brain for meditators is the decrease in size and function of unhealthy centers and functions of the brain. The amygdala is the "fight or flight" center in the brain and the storehouse for fearful and anxious emotions. When activated, the amygdala sends messages to release adrenaline and cortisol into the bloodstream. These are the stress hormones that can be felt as a surge of energy as the body prepares for immediate action.

The amygdala plays an important role in your survival instincts. In order to survive, whether in the jungle, as for our ancestors, or in modern life, the primitive brain has to be hypervigilant of potential threats. In order to keep you safe and alive, your amygdala is hardwired to err on the side of sensing potential threats that in reality are not, as opposed to seeing things as safe that turn out to be threatening. You can survive, although uncomfortably, by mistaking something for being threatening when it is actually not, but if you err too many times in mistaking something that is threatening for something that is safe, your survival will be at risk. By default, your amygdala sounds many, many more false alarms than real danger alarms.

The amygdala's sounding of false alarms can be felt as the stress hormones increase tension in your body, gearing it up for the perceived threat. This can happen even while sitting by yourself next to a calm lake on a peaceful day—just within your mind, through memory or anticipation.

Regular meditation practice shrinks the size of the amygdala and, more importantly, reduces these false alarms, freeing practitioners from this hindrance. Furthermore, the "me" center in the brain diminishes, freeing meditators from the social stress of taking everything personally. Not only does the unwanted aspect of the "me" center diminish in influence, but the positive aspect of the prefrontal cortex for developing empathy for others is strengthened. On both accounts, this strongly enhances relationship and social skills.

Two Bodies

We all have two bodies, our physical body and our mental body. The physical body needs to be cared for with proper nutrition and exercise to stay fit and healthy. If you do not train yourself to maintain a healthy diet and you just eat whatever you desire, ill health will follow. If you do not will yourself into exercise and physical training of one type or another, the body will lose its edge. When you see those over thirty who are fit and healthy, you know they have trained themselves to stay fit.

The mental body is the same in that it requires training and discipline to maintain mental health and to manage the invisible yet powerful forces that drive the inner world. Without training, one is adrift in the currents of anger, desires, worries, anxiety, and distractions that can dominate the untrained mind. It is often said that the mind is a wonderful servant but a terrible master, and with meditation you are training your mind to focus on what nurtures your inner body and makes you healthy, happy, and tranquil. You learn how to say no to unhealthy thoughts just as you learn to say no to unhealthy food. You will yourself to rise up out of monkey-mind madness— to get above it all to gain perspective. It is like willing yourself to rise above stormy clouds to get to the clear sky that is always there.

A regular practice of meditation recalibrates your entire energy field by bringing your mind, body, emotions, and spirit into coherence. The physical benefits of meditation are well documented and numerous: stress and anxiety reduction, lowered blood pressure, and improved immunity, to name a few. A regular practice also improves concentration and focus, leading to better performance in all areas of life while also opening doors to greater creativity. With the diminished "me" focus of the mind, those who practice this inner art experience more peace in their family and social lives.

These are the secular and physical benefits of meditation; this practice brings peace and calm to the otherwise fragmented and distracted mind. For those interested in consciousness and spiritual growth, meditation is the doorway to the highest levels of spiritual insights and realization. It is clear that meditation could be helpful for people in all walks of life.

Meditation is the practice of calming your mind and turning your attention inward, ultimately settling back into spacious awareness within yourself. Unlike when you calm your mind to fall asleep, with meditation you cultivate an alert, very much awake level of your mind—aware even of being aware. This is a level of your mind that cannot be reached by thinking, no matter how intelligent you are. Meditation opens you to the space in between thoughts, and as the mind settles, the space in between thoughts expands—revealing the true nature of the mind beyond thoughts, like an opening in the sky beyond the passing clouds.

The essence of meditation is awareness. Following your breath, you rest in calm awareness, and then the wisdom and light from your spiritual essence begins to shine through. The meditative state allows you to become aware that you are aware. This awakening of awareness as your true nature is the meditative state. You are the observer of your body, and therefore you are not your body. To reinforce this awareness throughout the day would be to shift from "I have a headache" to "My head is aching," from "I am hungry" to "My body is hungry," for example. Joseph Goldstein, founder of the Insight Meditation Society and one of the leading voices in the meditation community, suggests taking this disidentification with the body a step further by shifting the labeling from "My body is cold" to "The body is cold" or "The body is uncomfortable," and so forth.

As you sit in meditation, you become aware that you can observe your thoughts coming and going, and therefore you are larger than your thoughts—you are something thoughts move within. You can observe feelings, sensations, and emotions that arise from the body, and therefore you are something larger that these sensations are moving within. What you cannot separate from is awareness. Awareness is always calm and peaceful by its very nature, and meditation is the process of coming to know this realm of consciousness within.

The spacious awareness that you awaken to in your inner practice is often referred to as the skylike nature of your higher mind—the original, pure, eternal, spacious nature of your mind when freed from distractions. While resting in awareness, you become aware of passing thoughts as if they were clouds temporarily obscuring but never altering the clarity of your skylike higher mind. *The sky is neither defined nor disturbed by the objects that move through it.* You are so much larger than your thoughts, or emotions, or bodily awareness. You are the space that all of this is moving within. Meditation is the process of training your mind to reveal this eternal, rejuvenating source connection within.

Higher Self/Lower Self

We all have a Higher Self and a Lower Self, and everyone on the path of consciousness growth seeks to be more in touch with their Higher Self. Meditation is the direct path to listening to your Higher Self. The Lower Self, the ego, is self-serving and always dissatisfied with the moment and seeks to change how things are in order to find satisfaction.

You can observe feelings, sensations,
and emotions that arise from the body,
and therefore you are something larger
that these sensations are moving within.
What you cannot separate from
is awareness. Awareness is always
calm and peaceful by its very nature,
and meditation is the process of
coming to know this realm of
consciousness within.

Meditating calms the anxiety generated by the Lower Self dwelling on the past and future or on innumerable distractions. In so doing, your own Higher Self's wisdom, spiritual insights, and inner knowing can shine through. Meditation allows you to access your own Higher Self, with its inherent qualities of peaceful awareness, spiritual wisdom, ease, and contentment.

Meditation Is the Direct Path to Awakening

In the Hindu cosmology, the aspect of your psyche that is active in meditation is called your *buddhi,* which comes from the same root word as *Buddha* and means "to awaken"—awakening to your own Buddha nature within. We call this the *Witness* or the *Observer* within. The name *Buddha* means "the Awakened One," and he taught that we all have this same capacity for awakening within. Your Observer is not just peaceful, it is also your source for discerning truth from falsehood—thus wisdom and insights are also gained while resting in awareness. This begins to carry over into the day, allowing you to stay separate from thoughts and emotions that arise. It gives you the ability to discern whether to engage with whatever is presenting itself (if it seems worthy) or to disengage with thought streams that seem unworthy.

Your Observer within is your faculty that is closest to pure consciousness. The characteristics of a liberated Observer are wisdom, dispassion, endurance, serenity, self-control, discrimination, and contemplation. In its purest state, your Observer is the seat of awareness and your connection to your spiritual self within.

It seems so simple: tune in to your Observer and you will awaken to the highest levels of spiritual awareness. However, your ego and the endless chatter of the everyday mind also influence your buddhi, dissuading it from trusting your Higher Self. The task is not to awaken your Observer—it already is awake; the task is to quiet the mind and senses so the inherent qualities of the inner Observer can come to the foreground.

Meditation is relatively simple to describe, and the techniques are also simple to learn. However, those who have tried to quiet their minds in order to meditate know this is no small task. It takes training to tame your mind to experience the benefits of inner contemplation. Your mind is the most unruly aspect of your being and requires training to free it from distractions. "I can't meditate because my mind is too restless—it jumps all over the place." This is often mentioned as one reason why many people think they can't meditate. This is normal and is the very reason it is needed. Everyone's mind is rest-less and jumps all over the place. That's the mind's nat-ural effervescence; it just thinks thoughts constantly. The mind's thoughts are like champagne bubbles arising out of nowhere, soon to pop and disappear.

There is a joke in meditation circles that one should meditate a half hour every day, unless they are too busy—then they should meditate an hour a day! This is a joke because for those new to meditation, even a half hour is probably asking too much. Start with ten minutes. It takes effort and discipline to get to the effortless pres-ence of the meditative state! By disciplining yourself to sit every day for ten minutes, your meditation sessions will lengthen naturally. As you start experiencing the rejuve-nating peace that comes over you from your ten-minute visits to this place that is always there within you, you will want to spend longer periods with the clarity and rejuvenation this practice brings.

Meditation shifts your attention from what you are currently aware of to awareness itself. As you deepen into meditation, your body and mind enter into deep relax-ation from the peace that ensues. Unlike in sleep, where your awareness drifts off, in meditation you awaken to a dimension of consciousness beyond the mind—pure awareness itself and its inherent qualities of tranquility, spaciousness, and deep acceptance.

Meditation: It's Not What You Think!

This bumper-sticker wisdom is a key for discerning what meditation is and isn't. Meditation is not of the thinking, self-directed mind. Although the dictionary will offer "deep thinking" and "contemplation" as definitions for meditation, this mind-directed activity is setting up an opening for your attention to move beyond the mind to what could best be described as spacious awareness: quiet, still, open, receptive, attentive, and aware.

Meditation comes from the Hindu tradition, and their word for meditation is *dhyana*. The dhyana stage of meditation begins as thoughts quiet through concentration on the movement of breath or on a mantra or through deep contemplation. As the mind begins to be tamed, you begin to open to a new level of awareness. Dhyana is a stage beyond contemplating, which is mind-directed. With dhyana you open to a level of choiceless awareness—alert, awake, and aware but not directed by the mind. As your mind silences itself, awareness expands.

One of the greatest gifts you can receive from meditation is to realize that you are not your body and you are not your thoughts. The first realization that you are not your body is not difficult to realize. If you are aware of your body, then the place within you that is aware of your body is separate from the body. You may even be a champion athlete, but knowing that you are so much more than just your body will enhance your performance. The second level of realization that you are also not your mind is a revelatory breakthrough for most people. To realize that you do not have to believe in every thought or emotion that arises is a great liberation.

Our Minds Are Shameless!

Our minds generate thousands of thoughts each and every day, from morning into the night. The vast majority of these thoughts are repetitive stories we tell ourselves to substantiate our separate sense of "me"—our "me" stories. With these thousands of thoughts floating through your mind each day, how do you know which are true perceptions and can be believed and which are condition-based, repetitive stories? As you develop your practice of taming your wild mind, the first step is to realize that you are not your thoughts. You do not have to believe the thoughts, doubts, or fears that arise from this huge data bank of possibilities that your mind presents.

The primitive section of the brain can hijack your attention with the imagined fear that there is something wrong, whether with you or with the situation at hand. With mindfulness training, you grow to know the nature of this primitive mind by watching the thoughts come and go and you realize their non-substantial nature. They come and they go, here for a moment and then gone. It is not that you are trying to halt this ceaseless mental chatter—that can't be done. However, you learn to see these passing thoughts as not necessarily true, and you no longer seek truth through the mind alone.

This is the great liberation that you gain from your meditation practice: liberation from believing your mind and emotions to be messengers of truth. When fears, doubts, and insecurities arise and you shine the light of awareness on them, they dissipate. Being in the *now*, just following your breath, can give you a sense of certainty and comfort while noticing that your thoughts and emotions are like clouds passing by.

This becomes particularly valuable when you are dealing with false stories about yourself of doubt, lack of worth, or not being lovable—pits in consciousness that you can fall into based on lifelong patterns and conditioning. When you are in the grip of one of these false stories, the tightening, darkening feelings of panic, anxiety, or dread can arise that you can't shake off. The story has you hooked. These stories require 100 percent belief in them to totally hijack your consciousness.

By practicing staying in conscious awareness of everything occurring in your body, breath, and mind, even while getting pulled into one of these pits in your consciousness, you break the 100 percent rule and the grip of the false stories begins to loosen.

Quitting the Habit of Thinking

Of course you can never quit thinking, and that is not the point. The point is to learn how to break free from the habit of looking to your mind and its thinking processes for your only source of truth. With mental training, you become the master of your mind rather than its servant.

Imagine if you were to sit down to your computer to do some particular research but your computer wanted to go to sites it was interested in. Would you abandon your direction and go wherever your computer wanted, or would you take control and direct it toward your intention? It is much like this with an untrained mind. You might want to focus on one activity, but your mind wants to lead you to things it wants to think about. Will you go wherever your mind takes you, or will you learn to take control and direct it to do your bidding? When you focus on your breath or your mantra, pulling your attention back to your focus each time it wanders, you are training your mind to follow your direction.

❧

In the following chapter we will explore the core components for training your mind that lead to the meditative experience.

Chapter Two

THE COMPONENTS OF MEDITATION

In this chapter we will explore the basic components that facilitate your meditation practice. These are the foundations that you can use as checkpoints throughout your practice and are particularly helpful if you begin to drift off into mental wandering. Staying mindful of these core components during your sessions will ensure success. Choosing the right time and place for your practice, what to wear and eat, posture, breath, concentration, mantras, and awareness are topics that will be explored in their role of enhancing your inner exploration. There are many branches of meditation that stem from these core components, but they all draw on these same roots.

Tune Your Instrument Before You Play It

Imagine that you are a professional musician and are running late to get to a performance. When you arrive at the theater, the audience has already assembled and is anxiously waiting. You can feel their expectation and readiness for the performance to begin. While unpacking your instrument, you notice that it is badly out of tune. What are you to do: rush onto the stage to satisfy the audience's impatience and play disappointing music from an untuned instrument, or take the time to tune your instrument and then begin your performance?

It seems silly to even imagine playing an instrument before tuning it, but how often do we go about our day without tuning the instrument of our being to the highest vibration that meditation brings? Engaging in meditation as a way of tuning your mental instrument before entering the world helps to bring out your best performance. Like a competent musician, the more you practice meditation, the more balanced, aware, and discerning you will be in the rush of the day's activities.

Choosing the Right Place for Your Practice

Creating a special place for your practice is helpful but not necessary. You can meditate in your office chair during your lunch break and achieve the desired peace of mind, but creating a special place dedicated to your practice can be very helpful. When you visit a sacred building, church, or temple where people have gathered together in worship, you can feel the sacred energy stored in the space. You can create your own sacred site in a corner of a room where you live that becomes permeated with the spiritual vibrations and intention of your practice.

Creating an Altar

Many people enjoy creating an altar to enhance their sacred space. Be creative and use what inspires and motivates you, such as pictures of those who inspire you, spiritual teachers who have helped illuminate your way, candles, bells, flowers, art, incense, and all that inspires a sense of reverence. Music is optional, and for relaxation meditations the right music can be very helpful.

What to Wear

Although you can meditate while dressed in formal attire, you will want to wear clothes that are comfortable for your daily practice. Doing a few stretching exercises to loosen your spine is certainly helpful before your session, and you will want clothes that you feel at ease moving and stretching in. The growing interest in meditation and yoga worldwide has spawned an industry providing special clothing and accoutrements to enhance your experience. All of this is helpful if it provides greater comfort and inspires a greater sense of reverence for your practice, while none of it is helpful if you think it is necessary. An important step in the meditation process is withdrawing your attention from the senses to explore your inner world, so what to wear is mostly a matter of personal taste and comfort.

What to Eat

To support your efforts to turn your attention inward, you want to minimize all distractions in order to pull your attention away from your senses, so you will not want to be too hungry nor too full. You don't want your body to be busy digesting a heavy meal, nor so hungry that it becomes distracting. If you are going to eat something before your practice, keep it light. There are many practitioners who like to meditate upon waking, before eating or drinking anything, while most prefer to at least drink their favorite morning beverage to fully wake up before beginning. Again, there are no hard-and-fast rules about what to eat, other than doing what works best for you.

When Is the Best Time to Meditate?

The question of when to meditate is highly personal. Many people like to meditate before going to sleep for the night, ensuring a peaceful entry into the dreamtime. Others prefer to do their practice after getting home from work to clear their energy field of all the day's responsibilities and pressures. Starting the day with your practice perhaps has the greatest benefit, because it allows you to enter your day centered, rejuvenated, and in touch with your Higher Self.

Possibly the best answer to the question of when to meditate is anytime—even quickies during the day to refresh your mind with little tune-ups are helpful. The advantage of a morning practice is that you receive the benefits of bringing your whole being into alignment before starting the day. Meditation is the surest path to awaken awareness, and to head into the day without awareness is limiting and unnecessary. Meditation turns on your headlights and helps you to see with illuminating awareness. You can drive your car in the dark without the headlights on, but the stress of this scenario could easily be remedied by turning on the lights.

Posture

The fundamental issue concerning posture is that the spine should be straight and erect, as if there were a weight pulling your tailbone down and a string pulling your head up. Although this alignment can be achieved while lying down, sitting postures are preferred, because meditating while lying down too easily induces sleep. Of course, in the middle of a sleepless night, this might be exactly what is needed! There are many people who have difficulty with sitting postures, so lying down is still their preferred posture, and this is perfectly all right. If you do tend to drift off while lying down, make subtle adjustments in your body, like squeezing your buttocks muscles or clenching your hands and feet, to bring yourself back to alertness.

Patanjali, who is revered as an authority on meditation, states in his classic text *Yoga Sutra* that one's meditation posture must be comfortable enough to allow sustained periods of keeping the spine erect. Trying to sit in a posture that is unbearably uncomfortable is counterproductive to reaching the calm state of meditation.

Although there is considerable benefit in learning to sit in a crossed-legged lotus or half-lotus posture, sitting in a chair with your spine straight is perfectly sufficient for meditation. While sitting in a chair, it is best to sit erect, without any back support. If you need the support, use it, but willing yourself to sit tall and straight is an important part of right posture.

Other tips on posture to fine-tune your experience include keeping your chin level with the floor, your ears above your spine, and your jaw and shoulders relaxed. As a checkpoint during your meditation, feel your sitting bones firmly on the chair, cushion, or floor, and lift your spine up from this firm foundation. Feel as if you are creating a little more space between each vertebra while still keeping your shoulders relaxed.

Being aware of your posture throughout the day can help you maintain strong positive energy. Whether you are sitting or standing, periodically check to see if you are hunched over, Gollum-like, which darkens your energy field, and make the adjustments to be tall and straight, with your chest open and your head level with your spine. Making just these adjustments to your posture throughout the day can do a great deal to help you stay strong and confident.

Breath

Breath is a key resource in meditation. Although breathing occurs with or without your attention all day long, focused attention on breathing is the surest method of quieting your mind and calming your body. By focusing your attention on your breathing, you bring your mind back to the here and now, and there is nothing more immediate than your current breath.

There are many techniques for using breath to facilitate meditation, which will be covered in the section on *pranayama* later in this chapter, but begin with the basic practice of watching your breath as you breathe all the way down into your belly and then observe your slow, natural, easy outbreath. Repeat. Repeat. Repeat. That's it: breathe in, breathe out—while holding your attention on your breath only. When the mind wanders, and it will, notice the distraction and gently pull your attention back to the subtle rising and falling of your energy field with your changing breaths. While returning to your focus, the emphasis is on soft and gentle attention rather than hard, strict discipline. Some people like to count their breaths to ten and then start over again, or to just think the word *in*, pause, and then think the word *out*.

Within just a few minutes of this practice, you begin to tame the restless mind and the distractions become less and less frequent. Even while in deep meditation, it will happen that you lose the edge of your focused attention, and when this occurs, go back to your posture and your breath to regain your edge. After sitting for a while, the body tends to relax, which is good, but not if the posture is sacrificed. After making any subtle adjustments to your posture, refocus your attention on your breath to bring yourself back into the present moment.

Slowly, as you watch your breathing and gently pull your attention back from wandering thoughts, your mind will calm down. Eventually, as you continue to practice, there will be a quiet space between the thoughts that arise, and in that moment there is peace.

When I played basketball in high school, I usually performed better in practice than I did during the games, much to my dismay. It wasn't that I was nervous but that I would get overly excited during the games, with the same damaging effect: breathing as fast as a jack rabbit, with a racing heart rate, inhibited my ability to perform well. After high school I found yoga and meditation and learned to center myself with deep, steady breathing. I continued playing in adult basketball leagues and was

As the body and mind relax,
the restfulness that ensues
is a familiar signal to your psyche
to drift into slumber,
and this you must overcome.
When this occurs, pull your
attention back to your breath,
your spine, and your posture,
making any subtle adjustments
necessary to bring you
back to alert awareness.

amazed at how my meditation training of deepening and steadying my breathing was benefiting my game-day performance, and I lamented that none of my coaches in high school had taught me how to breathe properly to stay grounded during the games.

Later, when I became a coach of my son's little league baseball teams, I was able to help many young, overly excited and anxious players improve their performance and enjoyment of the game by teaching them how to breathe properly—and to visualize getting a hit rather than focusing on not striking out. We learn in meditation that *where attention goes, energy flows.* With too much attention on not striking out, all the energy is still about striking out. Redirecting the young players to visualize how they wanted to hit the ball made a big difference.

Drowsiness

Drowsiness is one of the obstacles you have to overcome to stay alert during your meditation practice. As the body and mind relax, the restfulness that ensues is a familiar signal to your psyche to drift into slumber, and this you must overcome. When this occurs, pull your attention back to your breath, your spine, and your posture, making any subtle adjustments necessary to bring you back to alert awareness. It requires will and effort to stay in the state of effortless presence, which is one of the paradoxes of meditation. You are relaxing your body and mind, but your awareness is becoming more alert and awake.

• EXERCISE 1 •

Focusing on Your Breath to Quiet Your Mind

The first stage of meditation is concentration—training the mind to stay focused on a single object for an extended duration of time. Breath is often used because of its accessibility, its connection to *prana* (the universal life force), and its ability to bring you back to the present moment—and there is nothing more immediate than your current breath. As you practice this first breathing exercise, pull your inbreath all the way down into your belly, so that you can feel it expand slightly. This extends your diaphragm downward, allowing the major blood vessels to and from the heart to expand, enhancing relaxation in your body.

How long you do this first practice is not as important as simply doing it. Reading and knowing about meditation is not the same experience as actually meditating. You could read all that is written on the topic but not know the experience at all without actually meditating. If you only have a few minutes, do your practice anyway. Eventually you might build up to twenty minutes, but don't force that on yourself at the start.

Sit with your spine straight. If you can sit in a cross-legged posture on a cushion, fine, but sitting in a chair with your feet flat on the floor will work too. Bring your head into alignment with your spine, with your ears over your shoulders, as if your head were being gently pulled up from above. Keep your chin level with the floor, and let your hands rest naturally on your lap, with palms up to receive. Relax your shoulders, jaw, and mouth muscles so you can breathe through your mouth and nose with ease.

Steady your breath and deepen it in a controlled yet unforced manner.

Keep your attention on your breath for the duration of the exercise. Notice the subtle rising of your abdomen on your inbreath and the subtle falling on your outbreath. When thoughts and emotions arise, and they will, simply notice them but don't follow them, gently returning your attention to your breath. The goal isn't to try to stop the thoughts—they will always arise; instead, stop following your thoughts and return your attention to your breath.

Take special notice of the gaps between your breaths and the gaps between your thoughts as your mind quiets from focused attention.

Be gentle with yourself and try not to judge your experience. When your mind wanders, gently pull your attention back to your breath. Whatever arises, just notice it, but don't analyze it or follow it. Like a train car passing before your mind's eye, notice it, but don't follow it or wonder where it is going; simply pull your attention back to your breath. Picture your thoughts as having nothing to attach to, like champagne bubbles in a glass, rising out of nowhere and then gone. After several minutes of this exercise, notice how calming this is to your mind and body. Notice how much calmer you are about the pressure of anxieties or worries you may have been carrying before beginning this simple breathing practice. Now just sit with the experience and feel the effects. Enjoy the experience of now.

Whichever type of meditation you practice, monitoring the quality of your breath during your session will give you clues to where you are in the process. As you focus on your breath and settle back into your meditation, the breath begins to slow down. If you get lost in a thought or emotion, your breath will quicken and move higher up in your chest, giving you a signal that you are lost in thought.

Pranayama: Breath Yoga

Pranayama is the yoga science of using breath to awaken the flow of prana. *Prana* is the universal life force that animates all of creation. With pranayama breathing practices, you are focusing on your breath while also visualizing and feeling prana circulate through you with each breath.

Mystics know that on the wings of breath you can breathe anything into the body: love, courage, compassion, joy, clarity, etc. Visualize breathing in one of these qualities on your inbreath, infusing yourself with this quality as you hold your breath, then offer this quality to the world on your outbreath. The image of a dialogue balloon in comics can be useful. Put whatever quality you want in the balloon and picture breathing this into yourself on the inbreath. Experiment with the following breath exercises for activating prana and steadying the mind.

• EXERCISE 2 •
Alternate Nostril Breathing

Sit in a posture with your spine as straight as possible. Put your left hand in your lap, palm up. Raise your right hand to your face, with your thumb just touching your right nostril and your ring finger just touching your left nostril. Let your index and middle fingers rest lightly on your brow, and relax your little finger.

Take a few deep breaths through both nostrils until you feel centered. Now gently close your right nostril with pressure from your thumb and breathe in through your open left nostril.

Hold your breath for a moment and then gently close the left nostril with pressure from the ring finger and simultaneously release the pressure from your thumb, opening the right nostril. Breathe out through the open right nostril.

Next, keeping the right nostril open, breathe in, hold your breath for a moment, then switch the open nostril and breathe out on the left side.

After several repetitions of this cycle, you can drop your right hand to your lap and continue the activity without the aid of your thumb and ring finger. At this stage, it is your intent and visualization that guide the breath and prana. Even if some air gets in the nostril you are not intending to breathe through, your focused concentration on the same path of energy as before creates the desired effect.

Now complete your meditation by breathing through both nostrils simultaneously, and visualize drawing prana in with each breath. On the inbreath, pull prana energy all the way down to the base of your spine, and on your outbreath, picture this life force radiating from your core, filling your entire being and then pouring out into the world. After a few deep, refreshing breaths, rest in your awakened energy field.

This exercise immediately balances your energy field and can be used, even in an abbreviated form, to immediately restore balance. It balances the left and right hemispheres of the brain and the masculine-feminine polarity of your energy field.

You can add visualization to facilitate the balancing of your energy field. An example would be to imagine yourself sitting as a mountain. On the inbreath through the open left nostril, you are ascending the mountain on the left side. As you hold your breath, you are at the peak, the center of your brow. As you breathe out the right nostril, picture yourself descending the mountain on the right side. Then move back up to the peak and down the other side.

The next visualization works with balancing the feminine-masculine, yin-yang aspects of your being. While you breathe in on the left side, picture yourself filling the feminine, receptive side of your being with the life force of prana.

When you breathe out on the right side, visualize emptying the masculine aspect of your being of all that it has been holding, such as anger, frustration, the weight of heavy responsibilities, etc.

Now reverse the process. As you breathe in on the right side, picture yourself filling your masculine nature with prana. Feel your courage and strength growing. At the top of the inbreath, pull your attention to your brow and imagine the yin-yang energies coming together.

As you breathe out on the left side, imagine yourself emptying and letting go of all attachments from your feminine nature, such as relationship issues, worries and concerns about others, emotional issues, etc.

To complete the visualization, center your attention on your brow and visualize the masculine and feminine aspects of your being merging as one.

• EXERCISE 3 •

Breath of Fire: Bellows Breath

Purse your lips as if you are going to blow out a candle. Pant intensely from your belly, expanding it and contracting it rapidly, as if you were a bellows stoking a fire. Your third chakra, the energy center at your solar plexus, is your fire chakra. Picture a flame in your solar plexus that your bellows breathing is stoking. This is your will center, your center of action. For a pre-meditation exercise, picture the flame burning away the slovenly, lazy, indulgent tendencies of your Lower Self so that your energy may rise up to your Higher Self. You can use this breath of fire throughout the day when you feel a little sluggish and want to get going.

• EXERCISE 4 •

Ocean Breath

Hold your lips in a loose *O*, and as you breathe in and out, restrict your throat slightly so that you can hear the deep sound of your breath. This sounds like ocean waves, and as you continue your ocean breathing, the sound relaxes your body, mind, and nervous system. This is excellent for those who have a difficult time following their breath. The added dimension of sound helps focus attention on the activity. This is an excellent pre-meditation exercise to quickly settle your mind, relax your body, and bring you into the here and now.

Circular Breathing

With this exercise you remove any gaps between your inbreath and outbreath so that it is one continuous cycle, like the turning of a wheel. First sit in a comfortable position and focus on your breath, getting it to gently move in and out with no gaps, so your inbreath and outbreath connect with each other. Focus on your inbreath and let your outbreath happen naturally. Ride the current of your breath as if it were on a turning wheel from your tailbone to the top of your head and back to your tailbone.

As thoughts and emotions arise, gently pull your attention back to your circular breathing, feeling the prana life force energy moving through you. Staying with this for several minutes helps you move through blocks and feelings of being stuck. This is also excellent for a quickie energy recharge throughout the day whenever you are feeling lethargic.

Concentration

Concentration is a key entry point into the meditative state. Concentration is training the mind to ignore all distractions and maintain single-minded, focused attention on a chosen focal point for an extended period. Concentrating

॰१

Concentration is a key entry point
into the meditative state.
Concentration is training the mind
to ignore all distractions and maintain
single-minded, focused attention
on a chosen focal point
for an extended period.
Concentrating on your breath,
a mantra, a candle,
a photo of an inspirational teacher,
a sacred poem, or a lofty concept
such as love, contentment,
or compassion will work
for focusing your mind.

on your breath, a mantra, a candle, a photo of an inspirational teacher, a sacred poem, or a lofty concept such as love, contentment, or compassion will work for focusing your mind. Maintaining single-minded attention is no small task and improves with practice, practice, and more practice. Developing your discipline of lengthening the amount of time you can stay focused on your primary object will deepen your meditation practice and improve your concentration throughout the day in your other activities.

The dizzying amount of information coming at us from all directions in our modern world can leave us feeling fragmented at the end of the day. Steadying the mind through training it to dispel all distractions and stay focused only on the object of your concentration is a perfect antidote for staying centered in our chaotic world.

Mantras

Chanting a mantra is another direct path to clearing the mind of unwanted thoughts and tuning it to a higher vibration. A *mantra* is a phrase uttered over and over again, audibly or inwardly, as a meditative focus. Using a mantra is a technique for liberating the mind from its negative tendencies. Chanting *Om*, sometimes spelled

Aum, is an example. Chanting this sacred sound opens you up to high-level spiritual vibrations.

Repeating a mantra creates a mental vibration that allows you to liberate yourself from mental agitation by entering into the sound vibration of the mantra. Continuing to chant the mantra itself begins to melt into the background as you merge with the vibration and your intention. As you develop a personal connection to your mantra, it becomes like a tuning fork, accelerating your liberation from your mind's chatter. Using a mantra is an excellent way to begin your meditation sessions, as it immediately stops the chatter and attunes your attention to your inner world. Silently chanting your mantra during the day when you feel a need to stop thinking about something you can't let go of is an excellent method for triggering the neural network that quickly brings you back into present awareness.

Choosing Your Mantra

Eventually you will want to choose a mantra that you can stick with, so choose something that has special significance for you. Experiment with some of the popular mantras and see if one resonates with you, whether you like the meaning associated with the mantra or you just like saying it. Here are some of the more commonly used mantras:

OM: This mantra, also spelled *Aum*, is the original sound of the universe, carrying the vibration of universal consciousness.

OM MANI PADME HUM: (Pronounced *Om, Ma-nee, Pod-may, Hoom.*) This mantra translates to "Hail to the jewel in the lotus flower of the heart; I am that," with the lotus flower being the Buddha of Compassion in your heart.

OM NAMAH SHIVAYA: (Pronounced *Om, Nah-mah, She-vie-yah.*) This Hindu mantra means "I bow to Shiva," the supreme deity of transformation and gateway to the Higher Self. A modern translation of this mantra is "I honor the divinity within myself."

OM SHANTI SHANTI SHANTI: This mantra invokes the divine home within to establish peace of body, peace of mind, peace of speech.

GATE GATE PARAGATE PARASAMGATE BODHI SVAHA: (Gate is pronounced *Gah-tay.*) This Buddhist chant means "Gone, gone, gone beyond, gone utterly beyond, hail enlightenment."

SAT CHIT ANANDA: This mantra means "existence, consciousness, bliss."

SO HAM: (Also pronounced *So-hum*.) This is considered a universal mantra in that it already exists within the sounds of your breath. *Sooo* is the inbreath, and *haaamm* is the sound of the outbreath. Its meaning is "I am that," pointing to the divine within you.

Beyond being a meditation technique, your mantra can be quite useful throughout the day when you find yourself drifting toward negative thinking while standing in line, while stuck in traffic, or when someone is saying something irritating and you don't want to react in knee-jerk fashion to their negativity.

Japa is the practice of repeating the name of God in any language over and over again as a method for invoking divine grace. Jesus, Allah, Dios, Yahweh, Jehovah, Ram, Holy Lord, and Shiva are examples. Japa is one of the most powerful techniques for dispelling fear and negative thoughts. This can be done either audibly, or with just the lips moving without sound, or silently within. It is more powerful to practice japa silently, but it is also more difficult to tame your mind at the same time.

Awareness

The flowering of meditation is awareness, which blossoms from the previous steps of posture, breath, and concentration. After concentrating on your breath for a number of minutes, your mind begins to settle and you become aware of a little space between you and the thoughts that come and go. As this space grows, you become aware that if you can see your thoughts, then you are something larger than them. This is the great liberation that comes from meditation: you become liberated from a mind-encapsulated experience of life and become aware of awareness itself as your true, unchanging nature. Awareness is the essence of meditation. *Awareness hasn't aged or been wounded or tarnished by life in any way, and resting in awareness rejuvenates your entire energy field.*

As you open to the level of receptive awareness, it complements the active, directed level of meditation, and awareness begins to blossom of its own accord. You cannot make this happen; it happens naturally on its own and in its own time. As it begins, you start shifting your attention from *focused attention* to *receptive awareness* and the spaciousness and openness that attend the experience.

The concentration level is necessary to stabilize the mind, and as it does, receptive awareness begins to blossom, expanding your inner ability to explore your consciousness and the nature of your mind itself. Loosen the grip of your concentration as you sense this spaciousness between you and your thoughts and explore this space within.

Inherent Qualities of Awakened Awareness

There are several inherent qualities of awakened awareness that blossom of their own accord, without any effort. Awakened awareness is in the present moment, non-reactionary, calm, peaceful, and compassionate, and is the womb for spiritual insights.

In the Present Moment

The great teachings in *The Power of Now* by Eckhart Tolle and *Be Here Now* by Ram Dass reveal the tremendous value and peace of mind that come from keeping your mind and attention on this immediate moment. But this is not the nature of your everyday mind, which jumps forward and backward in time like a time traveler and is always, always anxiety-making. We know not to dwell on the past or be worried about the future, but this is exactly what the everyday mind does, and our efforts to stop this annoying tendency seem futile.

As you cultivate your ability to abide in awareness, this tendency to time-travel falls away of its own accord because awareness exists only in present time—inherently and always. You do not have to quit thinking about the past and future; simply awaken to awareness and it already is, and only is, in present time—here and now.

Non-Reactionary

When we are in a state of awakened awareness, we see things in the world as they are, without judgment. It is said that it is easy to be at peace on a mountaintop but is difficult to be at peace in a marketplace. We do not live alone or in isolation, and how often it is that our peace of mind is interrupted by our reaction to others and events in the world? We may wish we were not so reactionary so that we could hold our peaceful ground in the presence of others, but it is our everyday mind's inherent tendency to judge and evaluate everything and everybody based on how they fit into our ego's existing beliefs. The ego always, always sees the world as imperfect and not to its ultimate liking, and thus it is futile to try to stop this judging, evaluating, and reactionary mental tendency.

By cultivating awareness, you will still be aware of this tendency, but awareness is inherently non-reactionary and is peacefully observing all the contradictions and polarities as the natural way that things are in the manifest world. Awareness sees from the perspective of *this and that too.* Awareness holds all polarities within the oneness of all life, and cultivating awareness creates a little gap between the reactionary tendency and acting on it. This little gap of mindfulness is non-reactionary by nature and frees you from being tugged and pulled from your center by others and the world around you.

When the reactionary impulse to act or speak based on something another person said arises in the moment, by staying anchored in awareness you are able to watch it rise and subside. Being able to observe this while it is occurring allows you to make your choices based on your Higher Self's knowing rather than your ego's reacting.

Let's say you have been meditating for a while and you have become aware that you need to work on your anger issues—you get mad far too easily and would like to work on it. By changing your focus to what is actually occurring within you rather than whatever issues you are reacting to, you develop a new freedom of how you choose to react. With awakened awareness, you are keenly aware of every sensation in your body and begin to watch the physical sensations within you as your anger heats up. Learn your indicators by closely watching what is going on in your body: Is your solar plexus tightening and feeling hot? Is your breath quickening? How does the energy feel in your hands?

Just by staying consciously aware of what is occurring within you, you are no longer vulnerable to unconsciously reacting to the situation—you have maintained your conscious awareness and can make conscious choices as to how to respond.

Calm and Peaceful

Awareness is calm, serene, and peaceful in and of itself, like the sky. Just as passing clouds do not disrupt the sky, passing moods and thoughts do not disrupt awareness. Instead of cultivating a peaceful and calm temperament, cultivate awareness and this quality is already present— and it is always present. *The serenity that we seek in meditation is always there.* This is will be affirmed to you through the experience of feeling agitated, impatient, and scattered on certain days before your meditation session, yet even then you find that meditation always leads to the serenity that comes from quieting the mind.

Compassionate

We may understand the wisdom of loving thy neighbor as thyself and wish to be kinder in our dealings with others, but the ego's nature is to be self-protective and territorial and therefore treats others as potentially threatening. Cultivating awareness awakens your compassion for others because the inherent nature of awareness is to see all others with an open and understanding heart. Awareness isn't responding from your "me" center; thus, kindness, compassion, and interest in the lives of others naturally flourish of their own accord.

Spiritual Insights

Cultivating awareness affords you access to your own higher mind's inherent wisdom, and meditators learn to turn to their inner knowing when faced with difficult choices. You may be worried about a problem that has presented itself and find yourself anxiously lying awake at night seeking the right solution. Train yourself to meditate first and consider the problem from your awakened awareness, and then the clarity of knowing what to do will reveal itself.

Spiritual insights into your own nature can be revealed spontaneously while you are resting in awareness. You

Spiritual insights into your own nature
can be revealed spontaneously while
you are resting in awareness.
You begin to see the mechanics
of your own mind, often
receiving insights into how
your mind and your attachments
have been the source of
many of your own troubles.
It is like sitting with a
wise spiritual advisor who is
sharing precious insights
into the workings of your mind.

begin to see the mechanics of your own mind, often receiving insights into how your mind and your attachments have been the source of many of your own troubles. It is like sitting with a wise spiritual advisor who is sharing precious insights into the workings of your mind.

• EXERCISE 6 •
Cultivating Awareness

In this exercise you will be cultivating awareness and specifically experiencing how effortlessly awareness exists on its own. First sit in a comfortable meditation posture and take a few centering breaths to get yourself in present time, then just let your breath return to its normal pattern without you guiding it in any way. Notice how your breath exists without any effort on your part. Notice any sensations you might be feeling in your body, and notice how your senses are operating without any effort from you. Notice how your skin senses the temperature that exists without your effort, and how sounds exist without your effort. Sit with this awareness of how much your body is being without any effort. Awareness is just effortlessly observing.

Now become aware of the space around you—sounds, sensations, and movements that exist while you are just effortlessly aware. Become aware of the climate that just is what it is today without your effort. Expand your awareness of you being on the Earth moving around the Sun. Again, this is occurring without any effort on your part you witness the changing heavens. Awareness is the one still, changeless place that is simply aware.

Now bring your effortless awareness to all of the thoughts, moods, and emotions that arise and pass while you are aware of awareness and the sense of alive presence that arises as your being-ness. Awareness doesn't need improving, as nothing can add or take away from it. Rest in this effortless awareness and the sense of being this alive mystery.

In the next chapter we will explore a brief history of the origins of meditation and how the practice has evolved in different cultures.

Chapter Three

THE ORIGINS
OF MEDITATION

Although meditation is currently enjoying a renais-
sance of popular interest, the practice has been
around since antiquity and has flourished in many cultures throughout history. The first evidence of meditation
appears in the archeological remains of art on cave walls
in ancient India dating from as early as 5000 BCE. Images
of individuals in the traditional meditation posture, called
tantras, reveal their understanding of this sacred practice
from the earliest beginnings of Hinduism.

Around the year 500 BCE, the Buddha made meditation accessible to the masses. From his teachings, meditation spread throughout India, China, and Japan and now throughout the world. Each culture has adapted the teachings and meditation techniques to create their own unique style, but the Buddha's teachings are at their core. A statue of the Buddha meditating graces many meditation centers and contemplation gardens throughout the world today.

Another pillar in the history of meditation is Patanjali, whose date of birth is uncertain but who is believed to have lived sometime in the second or third centuries BCE. Although the practice of this inner science had been around and taught through oral traditions for centuries, Patanjali was the first to compile and record the teachings in the revered book *Yoga Sutra*, which is still considered the authoritative text on specific states of meditation. Patanjali outlined one system of yoga called *eight-limb yoga*, with the goal being union with the divine in the final stages. We will explore these eight limbs as a model for understanding the various stages of meditation at the end of this chapter.

Swami Vivekananda was the first to introduce meditation in the United States in 1893 at the World Parliament of Religions in Chicago—an adjunct to the world's fair. From his teachings, the Vedanta Society began and still flourishes today as a center for teaching meditation.

Paramahansa Yogananda moved to the United States in 1920 from India and started the Self-Realization Fellowship (SRF), a worldwide organization for disseminating his teachings on meditation. (His Kriya practice is explored further in exercise 14 in chapter 5.) Yogananda was the first Hindu teacher to spend extended time living in America, working from the SRF headquarters and traveling the country teaching meditation to thousands until his death in 1952. His book *Autobiography of a Yogi* is a must-read spiritual classic.

In the 1960s, the Beatles stimulated an interest in the teachings of Maharishi Mahesh Yogi and *Transcendental Meditation*, the practice of chanting one's personal mantra as a method for quieting the mind and entering the transcendent state. This practice bloomed throughout the West, as well as the world, and continues today. Interest in hatha yoga and meditation of all types was seeded in the West at this time as well, blossoming into the huge number of worldwide practitioners there are today.

Ramana Maharshi is another highly regarded authority on meditation. He taught the purest form, *Advaita Vedanta* (non-duality), through the supremely simple discipline of self-enquiry into the source of the "I am."

D. T. Suzuki first introduced Zen meditation to the West in 1908, with an emphasis on *satori*, the mystical union with the divine. Shunryu Suzuki, author of another classic book on meditation, *Zen Mind, Beginner's Mind*, trained in Zen Buddhism in Japan, studying with Kosen Roshi. He felt a calling to bring Zen to the West, and in 1959 he went to San Francisco and invited the young people he met there to join him for his daily practice. From this modest beginning, interest in Zen spread throughout America. Instead of insisting that participants adhere to the rigid dress and behavior codes of Zen in Japan, Suzuki Roshi welcomed the young hippies with their wild attire to join him, supporting meditation teacher Eknath Easwaran's notion that meditation is a "come as you are" party. Easwaran founded the Blue Mountain Center of Meditation and Nilgiri Press in 1961 to publish his many books on meditation and spiritual living.

The Indian guru Osho, previously known as Bhagwan Shree Rajneesh, took this attitude of meditation as a "come as you are" party even further in his ashrams, where he encouraged an uninhibited approach to consciousness growth. This was a radical departure from the sedate ashrams most were familiar with.

Osho's teachings on meditation were also a radical departure from the disciplined approach traditionally taught. Osho believed that most Western meditators were not sitting in true meditation but were spending most of their time attempting to repress their thoughts and desires. To remedy this, he encouraged practitioners to begin their meditation with a mad, cathartic release dance called *Dynamic Meditation* to shake off and release pent-up energy. The teaching is that in the middle of the mad dance you become aware of the stillness within. Sitting in the stillness after all of this releasing also becomes much easier to do.

A pioneer in advancing the application of meditation is Jon Kabat-Zinn. In 1979 he developed a program called *Mindfulness-Based Stress Reduction (MBSR)* at the University of Massachusetts Medical Center. This was the medical community's first introduction to the benefits of meditation, and the program is now offered in over two hundred medical centers, hospitals, and clinics worldwide. Mindfulness training has shown to be an effective means of diminishing the stress related to being a patient as well as diminishing the need for pain medication.

Thich Nhat Hanh, a Buddhist monk and author of over a hundred books, was nominated for the 1967 Nobel Peace Prize for his efforts to bring peace to Vietnam. Nhat Hanh's teachings on peace in each and every step are fundamental to walking meditation, as illustrated in this quote from chapter 1 of his book *Being Peace*: "Breathing in, I calm my body. Breathing out, I smile." He still travels internationally teaching mindfulness meditation.

Joseph Goldstein, an instrumental leader in the meditation community, co-founded in 1975 the Insight Meditation Society, which continues to offer meditation training throughout the world. The teachings of Deepak Chopra and Eckhart Tolle did much to bring meditation into public awareness beginning in the 1990s and continue to flourish today. Spirit Rock Meditation Center, founded by a core group of teachers including Jack Kornfield, Joseph Goldstein, and Sharon Salzberg, has become an esteemed institute for insight and mindfulness meditation training. Adyashanti is another modern meditation teacher who has a global following. In his book *True Meditation,* he teaches letting go of all techniques and resting in pure awareness as the ultimate practice.

Thich Nhat Hanh's teachings on
peace in each and every step
are fundamental to walking meditation,
as illustrated in this quote from
chapter 1 of his book *Being Peace*:
"Breathing in, I calm my body.
Breathing out, I smile."

Patanjali's Eight Limbs of Yoga

Patanjali's *Yoga Sutra*, the ancient text that is divided into four chapters or books, not only provides precise distinctions between the different levels of meditation, but also serves as a guide to the practices that support a meditative lifestyle. The eight limbs of yoga outlined by Patanjali might sound like teachings on complicated physical postures, but postures are only one of the support limbs (the third limb), while the upper limbs deal with achieving union with the divine through deep meditation.

The goal of Patanjali's yoga system is to quiet the activity of the mind so that it may rest in complete absorption with the divine. Patanjali states in the second sutra in chapter 1 of the *Yoga Sutras,* "Yoga is control of thought waves on the mind." This sutra clearly states the intent of yoga: it is the practice of withdrawing the senses from all material and worldly issues to ultimately quiet the restless mind.

The first two limbs of Patanjali's eightfold path encourage right behavior in your life, so as not to create further karma, inhibiting the ability to be free. The next three limbs deal with the activities required to turn your attention to your inner realm. The final three limbs are related exclusively to meditation itself and reveal the stages of consciousness you ascend on the way to the final stage, *samadhi* (absorption). In samadhi, your consciousness is absorbed into what you are aware of, dissolving your individual sense of self as a separate being, leading to the realization of and union with your spiritual self.

1. Yamas

The *yamas* are the first stage of the eightfold path. These five main precepts are guidelines for developing self-control. The first yama, *ahimsa* (living with the intention of not causing harm or injury to anyone or anything), encapsulates the remaining yamas of being truthful, not stealing, expressing honorable sexuality, and not being covetous (not grasping or wanting). The yamas are the *don'ts* of the yoga path of meditation.

2. Niyamas

These are the *do's* of yoga, the ethical practices that support a meditation practice. The five niyamas include purification of the body and mind, practicing simplicity in all ways, cultivating contentment with one's life, and studying sacred texts to anchor the mind in the spiritual realm.

3. Asanas

These are the body postures most often associated with yoga. Asanas have been developed over the centuries and handed down through the generations. These postures have been specifically designed to help awaken the flow of life force through one's total energy field. For the purpose of meditation, Patanjali states only that your spine, neck, and head should be aligned and that your posture should be comfortable enough so that you can stay in it for a length of time.

4. Pranayama

This is the practice of controlling and using the breath to awaken the movement of prana, the universal life force. Breath is the vehicle that moves the subtle life force of prana through your body, and pranayama breath exercises teach you to control, direct, and enhance this vital life force. (Pranayama breath exercises are available in chapter 2.)

5. Pratyahara

This is the practice of consciously withdrawing your attention away from your senses and worldly concerns to explore your inner world. Pratyahara is the bridge between the physical aspects of yoga (the first four limbs) and internal yoga (the final three limbs).

6. Dharana

Dharana translates as "concentration"—holding your attention on the primary object of meditation, be it your breath, a mantra, the tip of your nose, your third eye, a particular concept, or an image. The same advice of gently pulling your attention back when it wanders from your primary object applies to all concentration activities. Training the mind to stay in single-minded, focused attention steadies the mind and calms the body. Many meditation techniques utilize this level of focused attention exclusively.

Practicing asanas teaches you control of your body. Practicing pranayama teaches you to control your breath. Practicing pratyahara teaches you to control your senses. At the dharana level, you learn to control your mind.

7. Dhyana

Dhyana is awareness. The Sanskrit meaning for dhyana is "meditation." This meaning of meditation is not the same as contemplation or any other level of self-directed mental activity. When you have succeeded at holding your attention with concentration for an extended period of time, a sense of spaciousness begins to be experienced, as you become aware of all the passing thoughts. Dhyana begins as you become aware of being aware. At this point you are advised to let go of focused attention and shift into the effortless presence of awareness— you no longer guide or direct your meditation or thoughts in any way.

Staying anchored in your awakened awareness gives you access to your own spiritual wisdom, and insights are often born spontaneously, particularly about the nature of your mind and how you have been creating your own difficulties. You begin to receive input from whatever you are meditating on.

At this level of meditation, from your practice of disciplining your mind, you become aware that you are not your mind—you become aware of watching your thoughts pass by like passing clouds. This is the second stage of meditation: awareness—you become aware that you are aware and begin exploring awareness itself, instead of the passing thoughts. With dhyana, you open to a level of choiceless awareness—alert, awake, and aware, and not directed by the mind. As your mind silences, awareness expands.

8. Samadhi

Samadhi is a state of absorption. While dharana is actively holding your attention on something and dhyana is a state of open receptivity, these two together lead to the final limb: samadhi, the blissful state of absorption where you dissolve into what you are observing, and in that moment you are one. You are enlightened, experiencing nirvana—at least for this one moment.

In samadhi, the separate sense of self dissolves and is absorbed into the oneness. There is no longer a separate person meditating, only oneness.

Samadhi is the realization that you are the awareness, the spark of the divine, the Atman within. This is the final stage of meditation—when even the gentlest waves of personal response to your meditation experience are quieted, so that absolute union with the divine occurs.

In samadhi, your breath becomes very quiet, practically still, as you are now drawing cosmic energy directly to sustain you, without as much need for your breath. This realization often brings insights into how you have created your own mental torments, and repairs the damage from living in illusions.

৩৩

The practice of meditation is a many-branched tree, with all the limbs drawing from the same root practices of quieting the everyday mind. The various lineages have all produced skilled meditation practitioners. Which technique is the right one for you is a matter of personal taste and style.

Now let's look at the various types of meditation in more detail so you can better determine what suits you. Over 20 million people in America alone are now practicing meditation of one type or another—so let's explore.

Chapter Four

TYPES OF MEDITATION

As we will discover, there are many types of meditation. In our exploration, we will group them into the main categories of guided meditations, contemplation, focused attention meditation, meditations for the heart, open monitoring with awareness, and gazing meditations.

Guided Meditations

With guided meditations and visualizations, you listen to a speaker or a recording guide you through the exercise. This type of meditation is particularly helpful for those new to the practice to help familiarize them with the experience. Following the guided imagery has the benefit of keeping you on track so you will know what it is like to have the actual experience. An excellent way of entering into a restful sleep would be to listen to a guided meditation while lying in bed.

There are numerous topics that these guided-imagery exercises can focus on, including relaxation, self-healing, self-forgiveness, loving-kindness, psychic development, contacting your guides, and opening to divine energy. Numerous teachers offer recordings that can be purchased or listened to online.

Contemplation

Contemplation is a form of focused attention where the primary object is a spiritual passage, a specific concept, or a teaching. Deep contemplation on sacred poetry, such as the Prayer of Saint Francis, is excellent for training the mind to stay focused on each individual word while contemplating its meaning. Contemplation brings the peace and relaxation that comes from taming the mind, and the rich spiritual insights into the meaning of the poem that you gain anchor its meaning in your personal life. Eknath Easwaran, a master meditation teacher, uses the Prayer of Saint Francis in a practice he calls *passage meditation,* utilizing a spiritual passage as a focus for contemplation. The following translation of the prayer is from Easwaran's book *Meditation*:

> Lord, make me an instrument of thy peace.
> Where there is hatred, let me sow love.
> Where there is injury, pardon.
> Where there is doubt, faith.
> Where there is despair, hope.
> Where there is darkness, light.
> Where there is sadness, joy.
> O divine Master, grant that I may not so much seek
> To be consoled as to console,
> To be understood as to understand,
> To be loved as to love;
> For it is in giving that we receive;
> It is in pardoning that we are pardoned;
> It is in dying to self that we are born to eternal life.

Read the prayer slowly, with the intention of letting the words and their meanings settle into your body. *Feel* and *think about* the meanings of the words. To contemplate an object is to go deeply into it, essentially merging and becoming one with it so that it reveals its meaning deep within you. Try not to be too hard on yourself when you lose your focus—you will at first, time and time again, which is normal. Be gentle and patient with yourself as if you were training a puppy to sit, and pull your attention back to your focus and begin again. The reward is that by sticking with your practice, even when you get frustrated with yourself for getting distracted, you will get better and better at getting further into the poem before losing your focus—much like the puppy that, with time, can learn to sit and stay.

The Prayer of Saint Francis is an invocation and an affirmation type of contemplation that you may wish to align with. A spiritual teaching expressing the truth of the way things are, such as the first teaching of the Buddha in the Dhammapada, doesn't invoke an intention, but rather affords an open contemplation on the topic and how it applies to one's life:

All that we are is the result of what we have thought:
It is founded on our thoughts; it is made up of our
thoughts.

Those whose minds are molded by selfish thoughts cause misery when they speak or act, like the wheel follows the foot of the ox that draws the carriage.

All that we are is the result of what we have thought: It is founded on our thoughts; it is made up of our thoughts.

Those whose minds are shaped by selfless thoughts give joy whenever they speak or act. Joy follows them like a shadow that never leaves them.

Contemplating this teaching that your life is coalescing around your thoughts can be a most helpful reminder throughout the day when you find yourself in negative thinking patterns. Ask yourself this: *If there is merit to the Buddha's teaching that I am scripting my tomorrow's reality with what I am currently thinking about, am I happy with this script, or might I be more responsible and creative with what I choose to think?*

You can also choose a lofty topic such as love, compassion, or wisdom to contemplate. Keep focused on the object of your contemplation and go deeper and deeper into your understanding and application of the principle in your life. If your topic of contemplation is compassion, consider what it means in your life and in the lives of others, and how you see this principle in the world. Stay with compassion as the theme, and consider it from all angles so that you may know its truth. You can study material on compassion from great teachers such as Pema Chödrön and Sharon Salzberg to further your understanding.

Contemplative Silence

Practicing silence is a wonderful contemplative practice. Absolute silence is nearly impossible to find, as there is always a creaking board, the hum of appliances, or the sounds of nature or your environment in the vicinity. Even when you turn off all the apparent sources of noise, sound permeates the ambient environment. It is better to think of silence as a practice of cultivating your quiet listening mind—silent inside, silent outside.

Practice listening more with your body and not just your ears. The vibration of sound resonates most within your ears, but your entire body feels the quality of sound vibration. Listen to sounds beyond your ears. Practice not labeling the sounds, such as "barking dog," and feel the sound waves move through you, or say to yourself *sound*, rather than considering its source.

As you observe sound waves moving through you, notice that when they are gone, they are gone without a trace. Practice this with thoughts—letting them arise, move through you, and then disappear without a trace.

Contemplating the Development of Virtues

You can spend time in deep contemplation of virtues that you would like to develop to help them blossom in your character. Let's say in your meditations you have become aware that you are more irritable and impatient with others than you would like. The opposite virtue of these agitations is patience, and this you will use as your focus of contemplation to give it fertile soil in your consciousness so that it may take root in your life. Instead of overcoming your irritability with others stemming from your impatience, by cultivating the opposite quality of patience, the aggravating behavior will subside on its own.

Spend your whole session contemplating patience itself as a virtue and how you see where it could be beneficial in your life. Contemplate individuals you admire who demonstrate this quality in their lives. Recall situations where your lack of patience caused trouble in your life, and then imagine how the situation could have gone better had you been patient. Picture yourself handling a similar scenario with the grace and ease that come from patience, and vow to aspire to this virtue today in all ways.

After practicing being a patient person for a day, spend time in your next morning's inner contemplation noting moments of your progress—where you did well and where you can see room for progress. Vow to improve on yesterday's performance today. Stick with this process day after day, evaluating your progress and then vowing to improve upon it each day until you have retrained yourself—patience has become so ingrained in you that impatience is no longer troublesome. It will still raise its head periodically, but it is easier to subdue through your efforts at retraining yourself.

Focused Attention Meditation

Focused attention meditation involves concentrating your attention on a chosen object as a method for bringing your mind back to the present moment and turning off your mental chatter. This practice is particularly helpful for calming your mind and relieving stress. Many people find this type of meditation easier than open-monitoring types, particularly in the earlier stages of training. This gives the mind something to do in the session—you have to keep remembering to stay focused on the object.

You can choose almost anything from any of your senses to focus on. We have already covered using your breath as a primary focus, with its advantage of always being available. A candle flame, the tone of a crystal bowl, a mantra, the smell of incense, the feel of a stone, a photo, or a piece of art that feels sacred to you are examples from various senses to choose as your primary object.

Start with shorter sessions of several minutes to ensure success, then build toward ten, fifteen, and twenty minutes. A key is not to be hard on yourself when you fail to keep your focus and find yourself drifting away—it happens. As when training a puppy, be patient with your progress to reap the benefits.

First sit in a comfortable posture, with your spine and head straight and in alignment. Take a few deep, centering breaths to calm your mind and get present. Then begin your session with the primary object you have chosen to focus on. A key is to directly experience your object of focus beyond your thoughts about it. At first it is you chanting your mantra or gazing at the candle flame, and as you stay with the practice, the "you" drops away as you merge with the object of your focus.

Walking meditation is another
popular form of calming the
mind and is particularly helpful
for those who have difficulty sitting.
As with sitting practices,
the intent of walking meditation
is to become more mindful of
the moment and not let your
thoughts wander aimlessly.

As you continue your practice day after day, you will begin to notice patterns in your mind's distractions that pull you away from your focus. These insights into the workings of your own mind most often come of their own accord, and you will want to sit and contemplate these nuggets of insight when they do.

Walking Meditation

Walking meditation is another popular form of calming the mind and is particularly helpful for those who have difficulty sitting. As with sitting practices, the intent of walking meditation is to become more mindful of the moment and not let your thoughts wander aimlessly. Thich Nhat Hanh has done much to promote meditation in the world. In his books, such as *Being Peace* and *Peace Is Every Step*, Nhat Hanh encourages us to incorporate meditation techniques of staying in mindful awareness throughout the day, whether we are walking, driving, cooking, eating, etc. We can practice focusing on our breath and becoming conscious of the moment. Nhat Hanh offers numerous little sayings that can be incorporated into your walking meditation, such as *Breathing in, I calm my body. Breathing out, I smile.*

We smile when we feel happy and joyful, but it also works the other way around: smiling makes us feel happy and joyful. The act of smiling releases the feel-good neurotransmitters dopamine, serotonin, and endorphins, which relieve stress and tension and lift your spirits.

With walking meditation, you are not walking to get somewhere; the purpose is to be with the experience in the here and now. It is good to slow down your pace and synchronize your steps with your breath. You might breathe in for one, two, or three steps, and do the same with your outbreath. Find your natural rhythm. When thoughts arise, dismiss them, just as with sitting meditation, and return to your breath and to the moment.

Become conscious of your connection with the Earth. Feel it beneath your feet. Add sacredness to your walk by becoming thankful for the Earth and its beauty on your inbreath, and with your outbreath send blessings to the Earth and its creatures. You can note the separate sensations of walking itself. Be aware of the sensations of lifting your foot, moving it forward, placing it down, and shifting your weight forward. Be present with all aspects of your experience.

The practice of staying mindful of all aspects of walking can also be employed during other activities throughout the day, such as vacuuming, doing the dishes, eating, and on and on. When wouldn't staying mindful of all aspects of the moment be helpful? Ultimately, all of life's experiences are opportunities to practice mindfulness.

Meditations for the Heart

Meditation gets us out of our head and reconnects us to our heart and spirit. The following practices help you reconnect with your heart in a world that has become progressively interconnected at the mind level while at the same time increasingly disconnected at the emotional level. These practices cultivate an open, loving heart, so that your life and those you come in contact with will be graced with loving-kindness.

Loving-Kindness Meditation (Metta)

Metta is a Pali word that means kindness and benevolence, and thus the practice is also called *loving-kindness*. This practice cultivates compassion for others, as well as greater self-acceptance and self-love. This is very helpful if you have been angry or irritated with yourself, others, or conditions in the world. As the Buddha's teachings remind us, you are what you think, and thinking angry, agitated thoughts all day leads to an angry heart and mind. Cultivating thoughts and feelings of kindness and compassion for yourself and others softens your energy field and opens your heart, and you start experiencing the world as a more loving place.

Metta practice cultivates feelings of connectedness with others, which can be so helpful, particularly when we lament that the world is so harsh. Loving-kindness practice is an antidote for the harshness you encounter and allows you to do something about it, at least in your world. As you infuse your world with loving-kindness, this becomes your experience; you begin to live in a world filled with loving-kindness. Loving-kindness is not dependent on circumstances and is something that no one can damage, tax, or take away from you, becoming a resource for you to draw on throughout the day.

• EXERCISE 8 •

Loving-Kindness Meditation

Sit in a comfortable meditation posture and a take few breaths to settle your mind and relax your body. Generate feelings of loving-kindness by thinking of a loved one, a favorite pet, or a spiritual teacher who brings you into the feelings of love. Stay in your awakened heart, and from there you will be sending loving thoughts and kind wishes to your human, mortal self.

The phrases you use are up to you, and you may choose to alter the following phrases to something more suitable. To begin, you can use these, which come from Sharon Salzberg's book *Lovingkindness: The Revolutionary Art of Happiness*. You can say these aspirations audibly or silently within yourself:

> *May I be free from danger.*
> *May I have mental happiness.*
> *May I have physical happiness.*
> *May I have ease of well-being.*

Jack Kornfield, a spiritual teacher and co-founder of Spirit Rock Meditation Center, offers these phrases for aspirations on his website:

> *May I be filled with loving-kindness.*
> *May I be safe from inner and outer dangers.*
> *May I be well in body and mind.*
> *May I be at ease and happy.*

The exact words and phrases you use can be adjusted to fit what works best for you to plant the seeds of loving-kindness within yourself. Keep repeating the phrases over and over and keep a fresh perspective, as if you were saying them for the first time, each and every time. Otherwise it can become a simple repetition practice, like the alphabet song. Keep a fresh perspective with each phrase, discovering anew the feelings of bathing yourself in loving-kindness. You are planting the seeds for becoming a more heartful, loving person with each phrase.

After you have practiced this for several minutes and have awakened your loving heart, extend this to a loved one or a special person who has been of great assistance in your life:

May you be filled with loving-kindness .
May you be safe from inner and outer dangers.
May you be well in body and mind.
May you be at ease and happy.

Stay with this until you feel that flow of emotional warmth between you and your loved one. Keep extending your heart circle by sending the wish for loving-kindness to your family, your friends, your community, the global community, the Earth and its creatures, and even people you have had difficulties with.

> *May all beings be filled with loving-kindness.*
> *May all beings be safe from inner and outer dangers.*
> *May all beings be well in body and mind.*
> *May all beings be at ease and happy.*

Practicing loving-kindness meditation can be particularly helpful in troubled times when the daily news confronts us with heartbreaking updates of atrocities that humans inflict on others and all of life. Loving-kindness practice is something you can do when your heart wants to shut down in hopelessness. You can feel so powerless, as if there is nothing you can do in the face of such daunting global problems. Yet returning to your practice of compassion and loving-kindness is something you can do to keep your heart open so that all those you interact with will be graced with the presence of a loving heart.

The world is made up of what collectively we each add to the mix, and practicing loving-kindness is a direct path that we do have some control over, at least in our own world. This has a ripple effect and connects us with others who are also practicing loving-kindness, adding this welcomed ingredient into the mix of human consciousness. Loving-kindness practice is a way of backing up this affirmation: *May there be peace on Earth, and may it begin with me.*

After experiencing the benefits of opening your heart and how much more effortlessly you begin your day with an open and accepting heart, this practice can be incorporated throughout the day wherever frustration and irritation typically abound. Waiting for others, getting stuck in a traffic jam or a slow line at a crowded store, or dealing with impossibly slow service at a restaurant are all familiar situations where your world stops and you are stuck waiting—the typical scenarios that provoke agitation. You are not going anywhere in the next few moments anyway, and using these normally frustrating moments for loving-kindness practice transforms the experience from one of agitation into one of peace. Repeat your phrases inwardly when you are enmeshed in these situations.

In my own loving-kindness practice, I like to anchor the passages into my being by transforming the wish for greater loving-kindness into an affirmation:

I am filled with loving-kindness.
I am free of inner and outer dangers.
I am well in body and mind.
I am at ease and happy.

Tonglen: Feel It, Bless It, Release It

The practice of Tonglen comes from Tibetan Buddhism and is based on the principle that we are all energetically interconnected. As in a hologram, where each part contains the whole within it, in the realm of consciousness, each of us is an individual cell of consciousness within the greater body of human consciousness and each carries the vibration of the whole.

Compassion, born from the interconnectedness of all life, is a core principle in the Buddha's teachings. We are all here together, and if there is suffering going on somewhere on the planet, we will all feel this at some level. Thus, compassion for oneself, others, plants, animals, and minerals is encouraged. Compassion in and of itself is a noble principle, but you must have tools to process your compassion, or you can get pulled into the suffering yourself, adding more suffering to the world, rather than alleviating it.

The practice of Tonglen gives you the tools to deal with your awakened compassion in a skillful and helpful way, so you are not carrying the suffering of others. All suffering, pain, anger, and negative karma can be dissolved with this practice. Sogyal Rinpoche, in his book *The Tibetan Book of Living and Dying*, says that this practice can help break our patterns of self-cherishing and remove personal negative karma.

Tonglen is a skillful extension of empathy. Empathy is the ability to understand and feel what others are experiencing from their frame of reference. Many people are naturally empathetic to the degree that they are not able to separate themselves from the suffering of others and find it necessary to avoid suffering at all costs. Learning the practice of Tonglen can help restore a sense of well-being in you and energetically help others in the face of suffering.

Tonglen is the practice of exchanging oneself for another—feeling directly the suffering and pain of another, and then doing the work of alleviating this pain within yourself. You breathe in the pain or suffering of the other person as if it were your own, and then picture the dark energy moving through you and dissolving into the emptiness of the void. You then return to your heart and breathe

Many people are naturally empathetic
to the degree that they are not able
to separate themselves from the
suffering of others and find it
necessary to avoid suffering at all costs.
Learning the practice of Tonglen
can help restore a sense of well-being
in you and energetically help others
in the face of suffering.

out the compassionate wish that the other person may become liberated from all pain and suffering.

Tonglen is the inverse of the practice of breathing in the light and breathing out the dark. With Tonglen, you breathe in the suffering, darkness, and pain of others, feel this dissolve into emptiness, and then breathe out light, love, and a compassionate wish that others may be free of suffering. By dissolving the pain of others into the void, you free your psyche from carrying any attachment to the pain or darkness you are breathing in.

You first picture the other person as another you. You essentially empathize with the person to such a degree that you can feel their emotions within you. Then you picture these emotions dissolving in the emptiness, and send back love and compassion.

Tonglen is a beautiful practice to engage in when you are with a dying person. It allows you to be fully present with the person and the truth of the experience while simultaneously doing a tremendous service.

• EXERCISE 9 •

Tonglen Meditation

This exercise has been adapted from my book *Western Seeker, Eastern Paths*. First, sit quietly and focus on awakening your heart/mind to compassion and loving-kindness. Once you feel this love and compassion, imagine someone you know who is going through a difficult time. Imagine the other person's pain and suffering as a dark cloud of negative energy.

Now breathe this dark, smoky pain into yourself and imagine that you are taking away the pain of your friend. Feel this dark cloud move right through you and dissolve into emptiness. Or you could picture this dark cloud of energy being dissolved in the compassionate heart of the Buddha or Jesus. In this way, there is no personal attachment to the darkness and it moves through you.

After you have dissolved the darkness, reconnect to your heart of loving-kindness and send this love, light, and compassion to your friend, picturing all of the darkness that was previously there being replaced by this radiant light. Continue this process until you feel in your heart that your friend's well-being has been restored.

Next, extend your practice to all beings who might be going through a similar difficulty in their lives. Imagine the millions of people the world over who must be going through a similar suffering at this very moment. Breathe in all their pain and feel it, dissolve it into the void of empty space, and then send out the compassionate wish that all beings may be free of suffering.

After practicing Tonglen for some time, you will begin to realize that we are all individual harbors on the same ocean of collective emotion. It is futile to attempt to keep your personal harbor clean until you realize the source of it is the ocean and begin the practice of helping to clean the collective ocean of emotion.

We are all interconnected, and practicing Tonglen gives you a technique for dealing with this inescapable reality. We can't hide from the suffering of others, and we can't push it away without it affecting us in some way. However, we can open our hearts and begin the process of healing one another, alleviating the pain in the world and thus healing ourselves.

Self-Forgiveness

After a wounding experience that causes you to build armor around your heart to protect your vulnerability, it is forgiveness, whether for another person or yourself, that opens the door to healing and reconciliation. Many people find it easier to forgive others than to forgive themselves over something they feel ashamed about having done or not done. Holding on to judgments about yourself restricts and darkens your energy field, closing your heart to its natural state of joy. Try the following exercise if you have been punishing yourself over some behavior or another.

• EXERCISE 10 •
Self-Forgiveness

Sit in a comfortable meditation position and center yourself by concentrating on your breath and following the rising and falling of your abdomen with each breath. As your mind begins to settle, recall the image of a loved one, awakening a smile in your heart. Now imagine that you are breathing in and out through your awakened heart, drawing loving energy into your heart and sending it out with each breath. While resting in your heart, you begin your forgiveness contemplation.

Contemplate some way you have fallen off your path and acted in a way you feel guilty or shameful about. Stay in your awakened heart as you see and acknowledge the trouble you have brought upon yourself through your own thoughts and actions.

From your Higher Self, acknowledge, accept, and forgive the transgressions of your mortal, human self, as a mother would accept and forgive her only child.

Compassion is born of forgiveness. As you stay in your Higher Self, accepting and forgiving the faults and flaws of your Lower Self, notice the feelings of compassion for yourself that arise. You can cultivate this compassion for yourself by contemplating the burdens, difficulties, and losses you have had to endure in your life. Have compassion for the trials and tribulations you have faced, again as a mother would have compassion for her only child. Extend your circle of compassion to contemplate the difficulties a loved one has had to endure, and hold that person in your heart, with deep acceptance of the pains and hardships your loved one has gone through in this life. Extend your compassion to those who have helped you along your way, and consider their sorrows and difficulties with your open heart.

Extend this compassion to your community and out into the world, holding with an open heart the challenges, losses, and sufferings that people the world over have had to endure. It isn't hard to find others who have had it even worse than you.

Close your session with a loving-kindness wish for all beings:

May all beings be filled with loving-kindness.
May all beings be safe from inner and outer dangers.
May all beings be well in body and mind.
May all beings be at ease and happy.

Open Monitoring with Awareness

In the types of meditation we have already covered, the mind is directed either by following a guided meditation, by focusing your attention on something (such as the breath or a mantra), or by contemplating a sacred teaching. With open-monitoring forms of meditation, you let go of guiding and directing the mind and enter into a state of pure awareness, without any inner or outer direction. Open-monitoring meditations are simple to describe but are usually not advised for those who have not had considerable practice in training the mind with focused-attention meditations. Without this previous training, open-monitoring sessions tend to degrade into mental meanderings and will not be anchored in the awareness that this practice requires.

Vipassana: Insight Meditation

Vipassana, also called *insight meditation*, is unique among the many styles of meditation we have been exploring thus far. With other practices we learn to withdraw our attention from sensations arising in the body to rest in the tranquility of the transcendent state, while with Vipassana meditation the interconnection between sensations arising in the body and thoughts arising in the mind is the source of investigation into the truth of this moment. Insight meditation aims for clear understanding of exactly what is happening within you while it is happening.

Vipassana meditation is the practice the Buddha taught in his original discourses on mindfulness. He taught that your breath is your principal anchor to the present moment and should be your primary focus, and then you note what sensations from the body and mental activity arise. With Vipassana, you neither suppress nor act on whatever emerges in your consciousness while you are focusing on the rising and falling of your breath. You retrain yourself to allow and accept whatever sensations or emotions show up, be they pleasant or unpleasant, with interest and an attitude of friendliness.

Use your breath as your primary focus, and when a strong sensation or emotion arises, instead of dismissing or avoiding the interruption, let it temporarily become your primary focus. Accept and allow the sensation with an open, investigative attitude until it no longer calls for attention, then go back to your breath as your primary focus and anchor to the present moment.

You are investigating your direct experience of your body's sensations, not your thoughts about them. Go into the direct experience and let go of words and labels. The naming of sensations and disruptions as a meditation technique is helpful for detaching from the body and emotions to experience transcendent tranquility; however, Vipassana is not about seeking detachment or transcendence. So let go of the practice of naming what is arising, such as *sound*, *memory*, *anticipation*, *desire*, *aversion*, or *worry*, and go directly into the felt sense of the experience beyond the label.

By being fully open to what is arising and subsiding from moment to moment, you quickly become aware of the transitory nature of all mental and emotional states. The rising and falling of your breath is in a state of perpetual change, linking you to the universal rhythms of change, movement, flux, and flow. The you that is breathing begins to fade as you continue to merge with the experience, and it becomes as if life is breathing through you.

Essentially, Vipassana meditation is a deep investigation into the sensations arising in the body, and your mental reactions to these sensations, just as they are. This will give you insights into the workings of your own mind, body, and emotional patterns. Observing your body as a field of sensations that you neither have to suppress nor act on, but can simply observe, brings clarity. Sensations and their attending thoughts come and they go, they rise and they fall, just like your breath and all of life: change, flux, flow.

• EXERCISE 11 •

Vipassana Meditation

Sit in a comfortable meditation posture with your spine straight and your hands either relaxed and open on your thighs or linked together on your lap, with your left hand on top of your right hand and your thumbs gently touching above your hands, forming an oval, called the *cosmic mudra*. Take several deep breaths all the way down to your belly, with the intention of calming your body and mind with each inbreath, and then release, relax, and let go with each outbreath.

Now let your breath return to its natural rhythm, and focus on the rising and falling of your abdomen with each breath. Focus on the sensation of each inbreath and out-breath. This is your anchor to the present moment that you can always return to when you find yourself lost in some thought stream. Continue with this focus until your mind begins to settle.

Let the half-smile of the Buddha come over you to enhance your sense of ease and well-being.

Now focus on any sensations of tension you may be experiencing in your body, and breathe deeply into the tight area on an inbreath, then release, relax and let go on the outbreath. Breathe soft attention into your shoulders, neck, jaw, and facial muscles, releasing, relaxing, softening. Bring your whole body into a state of ease and relaxation with your soft attention.

Now that your mind and body are calm and relaxed, return your focus to the rising and falling of your breath. When either a strong sensation or a strong emotion arises in your awareness, accept the intruder as a welcome guest and let it be your primary focus during its temporary visit—and it is always a temporary visit. Neither repress nor act on what the guest is offering, be it a pleasant sensation or an unpleasant sensation of discomfort, anger, jealousy, desire, fear, or unworthiness; just observe and notice the sensation arising in your body while the guest is present.

Insights are born in the workings of
your own mind from this practice
of deep acceptance of the truth of
this moment. By closely observing
the interconnectedness of your
body and mind, you begin to
free yourself from reacting
to the body's sensations.
Sit with this practice for
an extended period to gain
the greatest benefits and insights.
Vipassana retreats are ten days
of meditation for ten hours a day.
With that in mind, sitting for
a half hour or more is realistic
for your daily practice.

Insights are born in the workings of your own mind from this practice of deep acceptance of the truth of this moment. By closely observing the interconnectedness of your body and mind, you begin to free yourself from reacting to the body's sensations. Sit with this practice for an extended period to gain the greatest benefits and insights. Vipassana retreats are ten days of meditation for ten hours a day. With that in mind, sitting for a half hour or more is realistic for your daily practice.

You can close your practice by bringing your hands together in prayer posture at your heart and generating feelings of gratitude and loving-kindness, offering this out into the world.

Self-Inquiry and *Who Am I?*

Open-monitoring meditation with awareness affords the opportunity for deep investigation into the nature of your true self. With the practice of self-inquiry, you are investigating the question of *Who am I?* What is the source of this ever-present sense of I? With practice you know you are not to be found in the body, and with further practice you know you are not the mind. Knowing that you are not your mind and thoughts, the question arises, *What is the source of the I that is aware?* With this practice, you stay with this question and resist any words or labels that your mind offers and stay with the subjective feeling of the "I am" within.

Stay with this and go deep within as you track the source of your sense of I. This is not a mental exercise, and when thoughts arise, ask yourself *To whom do these thoughts arise? Who is it that is aware?*

As you sink deeper into the source of awareness with self-inquiry, you are turning this awakened awareness in on itself, and you begin to see the workings of your own mind.

With enquiry into the nature of your mind, you see how you have caused many of your own troubles by allowing unhealthy mental habits. You see patterns with awakened awareness where you have been acting from subconscious motivations, essentially going unconscious in some area of your life that has been causing problems. As you continue your self-investigation with awakened awareness, you see the many ways you have been the source of your own problems that have prevented you from living from your heart and from your truth. You see the compulsions, habits, and desires as pits in your consciousness that you can fall into, and you see how to avoid them in the future.

Becoming conscious of what you were not conscious of before gives you power over the previously unconscious behavior. These insights into your own behavior patterns that are born in your self-inquiry practice have real value when you are next immersed in the previously unconscious behavior patterns. By staying in conscious awareness, even if you get pulled into one of the pits in your consciousness, the part of you that is aware isn't in the pit, and you can begin to pull yourself out of the hole and guide yourself back to clear thinking.

As you continue this practice each time the scenario presents itself, it becomes easier and easier to dismiss the unwanted pattern. You actually are rewiring your neurological pathways, creating new responses to familiar stimuli.

• EXERCISE 12 •
Neti, Neti, Neti
(Not This, Not This, Not This)

Neti, neti, neti is a very effective form of contemplating the question *What is the source of I?* Whatever you can think of, the answer has to be "not this."

Sit in meditation with the focus of your contemplation being on the question "What is the source of my experience of I?"

Take inventory of the ways you experience life and ask if any of these are the true source of I. Ask yourself *Am I my body?* The answer would have to be no. If you can observe your body, who is observing? Ask yourself *Am I my emotions?* Again, if you can observe your emotions, then you must be something larger than your emotions. Ask yourself *Am I my thoughts?* Again, if you can be aware of your thoughts and the fact that you are thinking about something, then you must be something that your thoughts are moving within. Ask yourself *Am I my senses?* Neti, neti, neti.

With each question, drop deeper into the Observer, the Witness point of consciousness. Imagine turning the Witness inward upon itself, no longer looking into your individual life but now gazing toward the eternal Atman, the divine spark deep within your heart. Sit with the answerless question and feel the presence of the mysterious source of I within.

I like to complete the neti, neti, neti exercise of coming into awareness by becoming aware of what *I am not*, then following this by affirming what *I am*:

I am aware of my body.
I am aware of my thoughts.

I am aware of my emotions.

I am aware.

After silently repeating these phrases several times, I rest in pure awareness, expanding the space between thoughts and inner comments about my experience, simply aware of being aware. Now I am exploring the nature of being aware, rather than what is arising in my awareness and its unchanging nature. This awakened awareness is pure spirit, and not of my body, mind, or emotions, and as such, it has never been tainted or wounded by them in any way—it is still pure spirit, as it has always been. Returning to this place within me that has never been wounded or burdened by my life's experiences is more than restful—I feel rejuvenated by reconnecting to this pure spirit within, as if this connection is healing my wounds and lifting my burdens.

I feel this connecting with my spiritual essence as the surest way to recalibrate my entire energy field to be aligned with my core purpose and purify my karma from the mistakes I have made along the way. This is when insights are born into the nature of my karma that has distracted me from following this pure light within. It is when inner guidance of what I need to do to stay aligned with this light throughout the day is often revealed.

I like to close my meditation by sending blessings of gratitude to the teachers, guides, and individuals who have helped me find the light within. After I have experienced my awakened heart with gratitude, I then make a vow or commitment to myself to show up for my soul's purpose today and be willing to help the people and situations life puts before me.

Zen Sitting Practice

The purpose of Zen sitting practice is not so much to attain a transcendent state of consciousness, but to train the mind to observe things as they really are and to accept life as it really is. In so doing, one's own Buddha nature is revealed. The importance of always maintaining a "beginner's mind" in your meditation practice is emphasized by Shunryu Suzuki in his book *Zen Mind, Beginner's Mind*: "In the beginner's mind there are many possibilities, but in the expert's there are few." It is ideal to maintain this fresh sense of discovery in your sitting practice each and every time. The fresh mind of discovery is to be guarded and protected as a treasure.

The practice of Zen is based on the premise that our original nature is Buddha-like and therefore is not to be achieved, but uncovered. Your original Buddha nature is masked by the endless traffic of your mind occupying your attention. By quieting the noisy mind with your focus on posture and breath, the skylike nature of your true mind gradually reveals itself: vast, empty, clear, holding all of the busy traffic of the clouds yet remaining unchanged. As your practice deepens, it begins to carry over into the day, and you begin to become more present and attentive to the moment.

Duality

Transcending duality by understanding that duality is the nature of the ever-changing world of phenomena is central to the practice of Zen sitting. Duality and oneness can be seen in the breath. Breathing in, you are drawn to your inner world; breathing out, you experience the outer world. Breathing out into the outer world and breathing in into the inner world, there are two—there is duality—but in truth there is only breathing, with one changing into the other constantly. Both are infinitely vast—the outer world and your inner world—but in truth there is just one world, and your breath is a swinging gate between the two.

There is the objective world of phenomena and the subjective world of your inner experience: there are two, but there is only one reality. There is your perspective and there is my perspective—again, duality; but in truth there is just one existence that we each see a part of.

With *zazen* practice, you are not trying to achieve a special state of consciousness—quite the contrary; the purpose is to accept life and this moment as it is. The only effort is to hold your attention to your breath—nothing special. With this practice you become aware of your true nature, called *big sky mind*. Keeping an empty mind, open and compassionate, you find your own Buddha nature, your true nature.

· EXERCISE 13 ·
Zen Sitting

Posture is of key importance in traditional Zen sitting practice. You may have to adapt the following instructions to your body's limitations for an extended period of sitting, but here are the fundamentals.

Sit on a meditation cushion with your spine straight, your ears aligned with your shoulders, and your chin gently tucked in.

Fold your legs into lotus posture, by placing your right foot on your left thigh and your left foot on your right thigh.

Hold your hands in your lap, with your left hand on top of your right hand and your thumbs gently touching above your hands, forming an oval, called the *cosmic mudra*. Hold this mudra as if you were holding something delicate and precious, with your arms slightly forward, as if you were holding an egg under each arm.

For those who cannot sit in lotus posture, this same attitude can be adopted while sitting in a chair. The important thing is to own your body and accept the here and now—just sitting with time and space as one—always here, always now.

While holding your attention to your breath, ideas and thoughts come, and if you don't attach your attention to them, they quickly subside. You start resting in big sky mind, noticing the passing thoughts as passing clouds, only temporarily obscuring the sky, but never leaving an imprint or impacting the purity of the sky in any way.

Counting breaths as a method for maintaining concentration is often used with Zen sitting. On the inbreath, say to yourself *Breathing in, one* or *In, one* and then exhale. On the next inbreath, say to yourself *In, two*, continuing to ten and then starting with one again. If you lose your focus on your way to ten, getting lost in thought, start over with one again. Practice keeping your focus further into the sequence each time to help sharpen your concentration skills.

There is a joke told in Zen circles of a student who, upon hearing these instructions, raised his hand and asked the teacher, "How do you get to two?" It is likely that you will get further into the sequence than two before losing focus, but remember the joke and try not to be too hard on yourself when you find yourself having to start over and over again. With continued practice, you will be able to maintain your focus longer and longer. It only takes patience and practice, practice, and more practice.

Gazing Meditations

Most of us are familiar with the spontaneous meditative state that can come over us while sitting by a river and gazing into the current, or lying down on the ground and gazing into the stars on a summer night. Nature provides an abundance of opportunities to pull up out of the everyday mind and become absorbed in the wonder and mystery of life in the moment. Gazing meditations are doorways into the present moment.

Mandala Gazing

Gazing into a mandala and becoming absorbed in the images and symbols is an effective meditation technique for calming and centering the mind. Choose a mandala that appeals to your senses and that you enjoy looking at. As you begin to observe your mandala, relax your eyes a bit and let your vision become slightly defused to facilitate becoming absorbed into the mandala. Note any thoughts that arise and gently pull your attention back to the image before you.

Mandalas are circles, the symbol of wholeness, and this practice helps to integrate the many aspects of the psyche as well. All of the divergent themes of the mandala emanate from and lead back to its center, as all of the many aspects of your psyche emanate from and lead back to your center, your source.

Contemplating the Om Symbol

Meditators are familiar with chanting *Om*, which is said to be the seed sound of all existence. In Sanskrit, the *O* is a diphthong spelled *Au*, where the two vowels blend together. Thus, *Om* is also spelled *Aum* and relates to its meaning: *A*, pronounced "ahhh," represents the waking state of consciousness; *u*, pronounced "uuuu," represents the dream state of consciousness; and *m*, pronounced "mmmm," represents the dreamless state of deep sleep. Chanting *Aum* is followed by silence, representing infinite consciousness.

Om Symbol

Contemplating the visual image of Om can also be used to heighten one's awareness. The symbol is made up of three curves, plus a crescent holding a single dot. The lowest curve relates to everyday waking consciousness. It is much larger than the other curves, showing how much this dominates our consciousness. The middle curve relates to the subjective, imaginative state of consciousness, including daydreams and night dreams. The upper curve relates to dreamless sleep and a separate order of reality beyond apparent reality. The crescent represents *maya,* the illusions that separate the rest of the symbol from the dot, which represents a separate level of reality, the oneness.

In the next chapter we will explore using meditation techniques for various specific intentions.

Chapter Five

MEDITATIVE PRACTICES WITH SPECIFIC INTENTIONS

Along with calming the mind and body to enter into a state of peaceful awareness, the skill of mental training gained in meditation practice has many other applications as well. Although the following practices are more visualization exercises than formal meditations, they employ many of the same skills for connecting with your spiritual essence for specific applications.

Tune Your Spiritual Antenna Daily

Picture your spiritual eye at your brow (your *third eye*) as having an antenna that extends out into the collective astral plane. Imagine if you are given the gift of an extremely sensitive radio that can pick up broadcasts from all over the world, from the most beautiful music and inspirational talks to all of the AM talk shows, news, and static in between. The tuning dial of this receiver is so sensitive that it has to be adjusted daily to get the clearest reception.

Now imagine I visit you in your studio one day, and walking in I hear this awful static and screeching coming from the radio. The first thing you tell me is about how unsettling your day has been and that you just can't get focused. What would be my advice? The most obvious tip would be to point out the source of the obnoxious sounds—the receiver needs adjusting to tune it to something more enchanting.

And so it is with the spiritual antenna of your spiritual eye. You could have walked with the masters in meditation yesterday, but without tuning your spiritual antenna today, you will be just as lost as ever. You don't have to get to a deep meditative place each day to stay tuned. A simple morning affirmation of your intention to tune in to your Higher Self, made in earnest, would work: *May I be aligned with my Higher Self today and that which is in my soul's best interest and in the best interests of others as well.*

The following practices are methods for keeping your spiritual antenna tuned to its highest frequency.

Kriya Yoga Meditation

This meditation is inspired by the Kriya yoga practice taught by Paramahansa Yogananda in his book *The Art of Super-Realization.* Yogananda called meditation "practice in the presence of God," a wonderful attitude and intention to approach your inner practice with.

As a preliminary to the actual Kriya practice, it is helpful to first do a few stretches with deep breathing to get prana circulating in your spine. After enlivening your spine with a few stretches, sit in a comfortable position, with your spine straight and erect.

For the actual Kriya practice, first picture a hollow tube in the center of your spine running from your tailbone to your third eye. For your posture, sit with your spine straight and your chin parallel to the floor. Rest your hands on your thighs with your palms up. If your spine slouches or leans forward during your practice, straighten it to get the desired result of magnetizing your spine with cosmic energy. The purpose of this practice is to magnetize the spine by circulating your breath lengthwise around it and thereby withdrawing your attention from your senses and concentrating it on the energy in your spine. Your tailbone is the negative pole and your third eye is the positive pole of your magnetic spine.

To begin, on a deep, slow inbreath, make the sound *Ah* by expanding your throat, and feel a cool current of energy rising from your tailbone to your third eye. I like to picture pulling my attention up through my Lower Self and lower chakras and reaching for my spiritual source.

On your outbreath, make the sound *Eee* and send a slightly warm current of energy over the top of your crown and down the backside of your spine to your tailbone. Feel yourself open to the cosmic influx of energy, and allow this divine energy to wash over you, softening, melting tension, and purifying your karma connected to each of your *chakras*, the seven main energy centers located along the spine (see figure). Feel your outbreath as a fine thread of slightly warm energy moving through your spine.

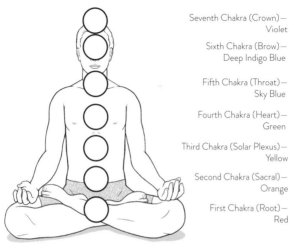

Seventh Chakra (Crown)—
Violet

Sixth Chakra (Brow)—
Deep Indigo Blue

Fifth Chakra (Throat)—
Sky Blue

Fourth Chakra (Heart)—
Green

Third Chakra (Solar Plexus)—
Yellow

Second Chakra (Sacral)—
Orange

First Chakra (Root)—
Red

The Seven Main Chakras

As you practice this continuously—cooling inbreath, warming outbreath—you magnetize your entire spine, drawing energy from the senses and transforming it into cosmic energy. This should be done 12–14 times to shift your attention completely into the cosmic energy.

Now let go of your focus on your breath and let it return to a relaxed rhythm. Inwardly chant *Om* and focus your attention on your spiritual eye at your brow as if you were looking out of it from the spiritual source within.

You may sit and simply be with the transcendent energy as long as you like.

To complete your meditation, take a few deep breaths and let your attention center on your heart. Be thankful for your experience and feel the joy of knowing this connection and the peace it brings, which is always accessible. Rest in your heart while contemplating all that you are thankful for and appreciate in your life. Now take a few more deep breaths and prepare to enter the day before you with your awakened energy field.

Yogananda teaches that the practice of Kriya yoga burns away your karma. Kriya yoga activates the energy in the core of your spine, called the *sushumna* channel. The practice connects you with this channel, which takes you to the place within you that is beyond personal karma—pure spirit.

• EXERCISE 15 •

The Microcosmic Orbit

This practice has been adapted from my book *Western Seeker, Eastern Paths*. To practice the Microcosmic Orbit, first visualize two energy channels for prana to move up and down your spine. The Back Channel, the receptive channel, starts at the perineum (between the anus and the genitals) and goes up the back of your spine, over the top of your head, and down through your brow, and ends at the roof of your mouth. The Front Channel, the assertive channel, runs from your tongue, down through the throat and neck, the heart, the stomach, and the genitals, and ends at the perineum. You complete the circuit by placing your tongue on the roof of your mouth.

The practice of the Microcosmic Orbit uses breath and imagery to move the invisible life force of prana through the circuit. First, sit in a comfortable meditation posture with your spine straight. Place your tongue on the roof of your mouth just behind your teeth to connect the circuit and start the practice. On your inbreath, pull prana up through the Back Channel, up from the base of your spine, through the spine, over the top of your head, through your brow, and down to the roof of your mouth. On the outbreath, picture the prana moving down your tongue and throat, through your heart and stomach, and past the genitals to the base of your spine. That is one round. Do several.

Use imagery and trace the movement of the prana in your mind's eye. You can use a ball of light, a wave of energy, a comet, or whatever image works for you. On the inbreath, pull the energy up the back of your spine, and on the outbreath, move it down the front. Feel this as cleansing and energizing your entire energy field.

After several cycles, reverse the process and breathe up through the Front Channel and then down through the Back Channel. Again, picture the moving prana as both cleansing and revitalizing your entire energy field. Feel the yin-yang dance of your energy field—the female-male, the receptive-assertive—and feel these polarities blending and shifting into one another on the changing of the breath.

You can do this practice for as long as you like. If you get dizzy or lightheaded, stop the practice and take a few deep breaths to steady yourself before you begin again. This practice serves as a general tonic to your energy field. Without discipline, the imagination leaks vital prana in its wanderings; with a practice like the Microcosmic Orbit, your ability to visualize is trained to serve you in a revitalizing way.

The Microscopic Orbit exercise is particularly effective when you are feeling overwhelmed by the chaos of life. By creating a circuit for the prana to move through your entire energetic anatomy, you liberate energy from the personal issues that are causing the feeling of being overwhelmed. When transformed through this practice, the same energy, which was previously overwhelming and chaotic, becomes the creative fuel for the higher mind.

• EXERCISE 16 •

Chakra Tune-Up

Sit in a comfortable position, with your spine straight. You can imagine a cord attached to the crown of your head that is gently pulling you upward. Keep your chin level with the ground and slightly tucked in and your ears over your shoulders. Take a few deep breaths to center yourself.

Now imagine the color red in your mind's eye. Any shade of red that comes to you will work. Imagine breathing in this color of red on your inbreath. Bring it all the way down to your first chakra at your tailbone. As you hold your breath, focus your attention on your first chakra and picture the red energy filling your being. Imagine the chakra as a wheel of red light, spinning, radiating, and filling you with this invigorating color. Feel the courage and strength of red animate your animal nature. Feel the aliveness of your body, and imagine being someplace on Earth where your body absolutely feels its best. Here, you can trust your instincts and know that you are safe and cared for on the Earth this day. Feel security come over you; empower your first chakra with trust.

Now imagine any shade of orange that comes to your mind. Breathe in orange down to your tailbone and then up to your second chakra, just above the pubic bone. As you focus on your second chakra, picture it spinning and radiating a warm orange light. Feel the joy, warmth, and pleasure of awakening your second chakra. Know that you are a magnetic being and can attract to you all that you need and want. As you breathe out, send this joyous, magnetic energy out into the world.

Next, find a shade of yellow that you are drawn to. Breathe this color all the way down to your tailbone on your inbreath, then on your outbreath see this yellow rise up to your third chakra, just above your navel. Now breathe directly into your solar plexus, seeing this chakra begin to spin and radiate yellow light throughout your being. Feel the power of your will, and know that you can use your will wisely. From here you can initiate activities and define your boundaries. Feel the confidence that comes from having self-control and knowing you can say yes when you mean yes and no when you mean no.

Next, move to your fourth chakra and the color green. Find a shade of green that calls to you in your mind's eye,

As you focus on your second chakra,
picture it spinning and radiating
a warm orange light. Feel the
joy, warmth, and pleasure of
awakening your second chakra.
Know that you are a magnetic being
and can attract to you
all that you need and want.
As you breathe out, send
this joyous, magnetic energy
out into the world.

and breathe this color down to your tailbone on your inbreath, then up into your heart chakra, in the middle of your chest, on your outbreath. Now breathe directly in and out through your heart, and see this chakra spinning and radiating a green light, filling your entire being. Feel the rejuvenating, healing energy of green. Your heart chakra is the meeting place of your lower and upper chakras—the meeting of Heaven and Earth within. Feel the deep peace, joy, love, and compassion that arise with this awakening. Empathy and contentment are also experiences you can awaken to while centered in your heart chakra.

Next, move to your fifth chakra and the color sky blue. Imagine looking up at the bright, blue sky, and breathe this color all the way down to the base of your spine on your inbreath, then see it rise to the fifth chakra at your throat on your outbreath. As this blue rises up your spine, feel yourself becoming elongated, as if there were a puff of air between each of your vertebrae. Focus the color blue on your throat chakra and see the chakra spinning in your mind's eye. Feel yourself become as expansive as the sky. Here your thoughts become clear, unclouded by desires or the opinions of others. Here you can speak your truth without it needing to be defended. Feel the freedom of your liberated mind as it sails into the sky far removed from personal opinions. Here you breathe the same air that has animated all creative geniuses. Pledging your intention to somehow be helpful to others with information you might receive, you are open to sudden knowing.

Your sixth chakra and deep indigo blue are next. Imagine the color of the farthest reaches of the Earth's atmosphere, just before it turns black. Breathe this color down to your tailbone on your inbreath, then up into your third eye, just above the bridge of your nose, with your outbreath. Again, imagine the chakra spinning and radiating this deepest of blue light. Imagine you are rising into the deep blue atmosphere above our planet and looking back at Earth with the view that we would have from the space shuttle. Feel the transcendence of this view. Your view is so far removed that you can't even see individual lives, only the Earth and its continents, oceans, and weather. Feel the bliss of this transcendence. Allow the sacredness of the moment to wash over you.

To stay centered here requires a quieting of the analytical voice. Just listen and observe. Thinking will happen, but pay it no mind; let the thoughts come and go as you stay anchored in your sixth chakra, simply observing. Surrender to any feelings of devotion for teachers, masters, and saints that may come over you spontaneously while you are meditating on your sixth chakra. Find the place of trust and faith that all of life is unfolding as it should.

Your seventh chakra and the color violet complete the meditation. This is your most spiritual chakra and your connection to that which is most high. Imagine a violet flame over your head. Picture it a deep violet where it touches your head, and as it rises upward into the heavens, picture it becoming increasingly more ultraviolet and then invisible. Breathe deep into this spiritual flame and pull it down into the base of your spine. Picture it cleansing and purifying each chakra as it passes through them. Then picture the violet flame rising through each of your chakras and ultimately out your crown and up into the heavens. Focus your attention on your crown chakra and affirm: *I am a child of God.* Know that beyond all illusions and appearances you have a direct connection to the divine within. Here resides the Atman, your eternal spiritual self, which has never been wounded or bruised by life in any way. Feel as if you are being absorbed back into the oneness of pure spirit.

After your chakra tune-up session, you may wish to sit in your awakened energy field as long as you like. To complete your meditation, establish the high intention of offering any good that comes from your meditation out into the world, so that it may be helpful to others.

Body Scan

This body scan exercise is an excellent way to bring your attention back to the present moment, and can be incorporated into the work day as a wonderful technique for getting you out of your head. This is also excellent for releasing unconsciously held tension in the body to bring it into deep relaxation. Throughout the day you can find yourself holding unnecessary tension in your neck, shoulders, facial muscles, stomach, or numerous other parts of the body, and this exercise will help you dissolve tightness and soothe nervous energy.

First, sit in your chair with your spine straight and hands relaxed, palms on your thighs and feet on the floor, with the intention of releasing all unnecessary tension. Focus on your breath and follow it from the tip of your nose to your belly, then back up through your lungs, heart, throat, and out your nose. Picture breathing in clear, radiant energy, then on your outbreath, picture yourself releasing and letting go all tensions, anxieties, and worries—at least for this moment. While breathing in, feel life's vital energy coursing through you, and while breathing out, release, relax, and let go.

After a few minutes of calming your mind, tell yourself that you would like to completely relax, and while keeping your spine straight, feel yourself letting go of all tension in your body. Focus on your intention to totally relax your body. With a deep inbreath, pull your attention from your tailbone to your crown. As you breathe out, feel a calming, relaxing energy wash over you from your crown all through your body and down to your tailbone. Do this cycle many times.

Now, with your awakened awareness, scan your body and notice where there is tension. Bring soft attention to melt any tightness or constricted energy wherever you notice it in your body. Breathe into any felt tension, and on your outbreath, feel the tightness release, release, release. Start with your shoulders and neck, where we often hold unnecessary tension. Breathe into the energy of your neck and shoulders with focused attention on how they feel, then breathe out tension, stress, and tightness, and feel them relax.

Next, move to your facial muscles, eyes, scalp, and jaw, first noticing their energy on your inbreath and then relaxing them even further on your outbreath. Do this with your arms, wrists, and hands, and after letting go of the tension, notice any sensations, like tingling in your fingers or a subtle warmth in the palms of your hands, as the subtle life force courses through your being.

Continue on to your chest, lungs, heart, and abdomen, including the organs of digestion and elimination, first relaxing any tension and then noticing the sense of aliveness in these areas of your body. Then scan your reproductive organs, your hips, legs, and hamstrings, and see if it is possible to relax them even further. Relax your feet, first wiggling and stretching your toes and ankles on your inbreath and then letting them deeply relax on your outbreath.

Now that you've scanned and relaxed your entire body, sit with the feelings of ease and openness that come with deepening your relaxation. Your body lives in the present moment, and in this moment your body is filled with awareness, aliveness, now.

• EXERCISE 18 •

Gardening Meditation

Staying in mindful awareness while gardening enriches the activity, lifting it out of the mundane and making it a wonderful practice for staying present in the here and now while also deepening your symbiotic connection to the Earth. As with sitting and walking practices, you establish the intention of not letting your mind wander, and use your breath to bring you back to the moment.

First, stand back from the garden and observe it with the attitude of being willing to be the garden's servant, tending to its needs. What activity are you drawn to while observing the garden with openness? Weeding, planting, thinning, pruning, cultivating, watering—what needs call out to you?

As you approach the activity you are drawn to, stay in mindful awareness. Tend to your breath and dismiss any distracting thoughts, surrendering to the needs of the situation before you. Try not to willfully do the activity, as if imposing yourself on the situation. Instead, form a relationship with the activity; let it be done through you. Let the plants and the garden inform you of what needs to be done. Trust that if you surrender to those needs, the skills will be drawn out of you to meet them. Gardening in this way can be a wonderful affirmation of the interconnectedness of all life.

Inner Gardening

Your thoughts and emotions make up your inner garden. Meditation is cultivating your inner garden: weeding the unhealthy thoughts, taking the brambles out by their roots, and nurturing the thoughts and emotions you value. Even if you get your inner garden perfect, without maintenance, nature will soon take it over with invasive plants and it will return to its wild state.

To keep your inner garden well maintained, stay mindful of what is taking root in your garden, even without your intention. Some powerful destructive emotions, such as anger and jealousy, are like blackberry vines, and you know they have to be rooted out or they will take over your inner garden.

Flowers in your inner garden of love, beauty, creativity, and compassion can be planted, cultivated, and nurtured into full blossom. The life force that animates these flowers into life is your attention.

The inner gardener knows that the life force animating this garden can be controlled and directed with attention. Your attention is your currency in your inner world. *What you pay attention to grows.* To *pay* is to purchase or invest, and when you pay attention, you are investing your life force into what will surely grow. If you pay attention to love, beauty, creativity, serenity, peace, and compassion, they will surely grow from your investment of your life force.

• EXERCISE 19 •

Self-Healing

In this self-healing exercise, you are first going to center yourself until you begin to feel the spacious awareness of your spiritual essence. Your spiritual essence has never been wounded by life or been ill in any way, and aligning with your spiritual essence is a powerful healing tonic you have available to you. After connecting with this revitalizing, healing spiritual essence, you will take this healing energy throughout your body wherever healing is necessary.

First, engage your favorite practice for calming your mind, and center yourself in the eventual spacious awareness that blossoms from your practice. This is your spiritual essence that is always clear, radiant, and vital. As you rest in your spiritual awareness, picture it as a ball of radiant light in your forehead.

Now breathe into this ball of light and take it to wherever your body calls for healing energy. Do you have a physical wound or illness? Take your healing ball of light to the area of your body where it is needed, and focus your attention on the ball of light infusing the wounded area of your body with its revitalizing, healing energy. Let this part of your being that is already healthy and vital help heal the wounded parts.

Is your wound emotional? Are you carrying pain of one type or another in your heart? Bring your ball of light to your heart, bringing light and the redemptive quality of unconditional love to your wounded heart. Love without reason awakens, and you can feel its warming presence.

Imagine this ball of light growing to engulf your entire being in its healing radiance. Rest in this radiance and feel the liquid light of your spiritual essence infusing every cell of your body with revitalizing life force. Know that every cell in your body being born in this moment is being encoded with this healthy vital energy.

Gratitude Contemplation

Using gratitude as the object of your contemplation is the surest and quickest way to pull up into your heart, and is not so different from the adage "Count your blessings." Focusing on what you are thankful for and appreciate in your life can be done as part of your sitting practice or periodically throughout the day for a quick heart-chakra recharge.

As Thich Nhat Hanh so poignantly reminds us, the conditions for happiness are always present, starting with

When you are not happy with
other conditions in your life,
practicing gratitude and returning
to thankfulness for these simple
gifts of breath and your senses
is always available.
Regardless of what is going on
in your life, there is always something
to be grateful for, and this will
animate your glad heart.

the breath. The fact that you are breathing at all is a condition of happiness, as those who have already died no longer have this luxury. The ability to see is a condition of happiness, allowing you to see beautiful shapes and colors and even to read this book. Being able to hear, sense, taste, and feel are all conditions for happiness that you can be grateful for, and that you would sorely miss if taken away.

These naturally occurring experiences are easy to take for granted, and yet when you are not happy with other conditions in your life, practicing gratitude and returning to thankfulness for these simple gifts of breath and your senses is always available. Regardless of what is going on in your life, there is always something to be grateful for, and this will animate your glad heart.

• EXERCISE 20 •

Ho'oponopono:
Reconciliation and Forgiveness Prayer

While my wife, Laurie, and I were living in Hawaii, we became acquainted with some of the sacred Hawaiian teachings on working in the realms of consciousness. One of my favorite practices we learned has the unique name

Ho'oponopono, which translates as "to set things right, back to their proper order."

This simple four-line prayer of forgiveness from the Polynesian mystery teachings is a powerful technique for bringing healing reconciliation within yourself, between you and a loved one, and between you and the world. At a minimum it can help heal your broken heart, and at best it can help mend wounds between you and others seemingly magically.

Ho'oponopono takes the principle that we are all interconnected on the spiritual plane and puts it into practice. When you do the deep work of healing a wound with another within your own psyche, this will have a corresponding healing impact on your relationship with the person in the outer world. Since we are all interconnected energetically, your Higher Self, called your *Aumakua* in Hawaiian, connects with the Higher Self of the other person, and both individuals will energetically feel the healing benefits. Here are the traditional four phrases of this practice:

I am sorry.
Please forgive me.
I love you.
Thank you.

When you say these phrases of reconciliation, go deep into the feelings that each line invokes, and picture sending this energy to the Higher Self of the person you are working with. Even if you do not believe that the problem between you and the other is your fault, when you say you are sorry for your role in causing whatever problem you are having with the other person and feel it in your heart, this opens the door for the redemptive quality of love.

When you say *Please forgive me*, say it to your Higher Self, to the other person, and to the mysterious divine source. As you ask for forgiveness, receive and grant the forgiveness from your own Higher Self.

Love is the strongest healing force, and when you say *I love you*, feel the healing energy of love move through your being and send this energy to the other person.

When you say *Thank you*, you are receiving the blessing of the prayer. Thank the other person for forgiving you, thank yourself for being able to heal from wounds, and thank the other person for sharing life's lessons with you.

Ho'oponopono can also be practiced with yourself if you are trying to heal self-inflicted wounds, such as a lack of self-care or succumbing to addictions or indulgences. Again, you use the same four phrases as when you are working with another person, but now you are speaking to your own Higher Self from your all-too-human mortal self. When you say *I am sorry*, you are acknowledging to your own Higher Self that you have fallen off your path.

When you ask for forgiveness, you are imploring your Higher Self not to abandon you. Vow to your Higher Self that you will listen to its guidance in the future and seek to stay in its graces. When you say *I love you* to your Higher Self, allow yourself to feel the heartfelt gratitude you have for your spiritual essence that has never abandoned you in any way. When you say *Thank you* to your Higher Self, be grateful for the forgiveness it has always offered you and will again. Be thankful that you can still grow and learn with its guidance.

Aligning with the Community of Higher Selves

Another practice from the Hawaiian tradition that I have found very helpful in my life is the practice of connecting with the Community of Higher Selves to align with their assistance in achieving goals and aspirations. The ancient Hawaiians believed, as many traditions do, that we all have a Higher Self, a Middle Self (our everyday, normal self), and a Lower Self. From these teachings, it is held that when you make an earnest prayer to your Higher Self to help you with a goal or aspiration that is truly connected to your soul purpose, it becomes your Higher Self's responsibility to assist you in achieving your ambition. It is further taught that if your goal is not just going to benefit you but would also benefit others, then all the Higher Selves of all those who could benefit from your achievement join with your Higher Self to assist you—forming a community of Higher Selves to support your efforts.

I was learning about this teaching at a time when my inner guidance seemed to be telling me to go back to school and pursue a master of science degree in experimental metaphysics. I was deeply involved with my astrology practice, meditation, and energetic healing arts and felt called to better understand the science behind my interest in the influence of consciousness in our lives. This all seemed perfect, except that my life was extremely full at the time. With four young sons, a commune and restaurant that we started, and my growing astrology practice, I could not see the time available. Still the call persisted, even after meditating on the question of whether this was realistic or not.

As I felt ready to make the seemingly unrealistic commitment to return to university, I meditated on drawing assistance from the Community of Higher Selves. I did believe that it was my Higher Self inspiring me to pursue this goal, and I implored it to assist me, with the attitude that "if my Higher Self is going to inspire me to pursue such a goal, then it is going to have to help me get there." I then surrendered to the faith that it would. I also invited in the Community of Higher Selves by affirming my intention to be able to more skillfully help others.

During the two-year program, I included this exercise as part of my daily practice, and I was shown over and over again its benefits. As part of my preparation for the day, I would ask that I be aligned with my Higher Self and that which was in my soul's best interest. I would then ask that I remain open to receive its guidance and assistance. I would affirm that if I was successful, I would be better able to serve others. I would then rest in the feeling of this web of support, and know it to be true.

I had only a couple hours to study at the end of each full day, and if there was an important exam the next day and I could not possibly read everything assigned to adequately prepare, I would first meditate on invoking the Community of Higher Selves and then trust that I would be led to what was appropriate to study. I would skim the text until something caught my eye as important and then go deeply into that until I knew it. At times I would even open a text randomly, trusting that Spirit would lead me to what was essential, and then study what caught my eye. My experience verified that this approach works, as I was, more often than not, led to study the exact material that was necessary to do well on the exams.

Healing from Being Overly Self-Critical

Many people suffer from being overly self-critical, from not being nearly as hard on others as they are on themselves. No one likes to make mistakes, of course, but those who are overly self-critical *really* don't like to make mistakes to the degree that it becomes limiting. It is as if these people have a "mistake monster" in their psyche that prevents them from trying new experiences for fear of making a dreaded mistake.

Everything in life has a learning curve. If you are learning a new skill or trying out a new technique in sports, art, or science or in personal development with relationships and social skills, there is going to be a learning curve. This means you get better at anything over time by adjusting and adapting to the errors and mistakes you make along the way.

Those who deal with the mistake monster would do well to adopt the following creed: *If I can learn as much from every mistake as I do from every success, there will never be failure.*

• EXERCISE 21 •
Taming the Mistake Monster

If there is an important goal or aspiration that you wish to push past your fear of failure to attain, first establish your intention of learning from every mistake as well as every success, and incorporate contemplating your progress as part of your morning meditation session. Contemplate where you didn't do as well as you would have liked and how you might be able to improve. Be willing to examine your performance with a critical eye for how you could improve. Vow to act on guidance you receive. Complete this exercise by visualizing yourself being successful at your goal, and know that you can get there, one step at a time if need be, by adopting the creed of learning from every mistake as part of a healthy learning curve. Be thankful for your progress and for the fact that you can still learn and improve.

Invoking Spiritual Grace

When your intention for your inner work is to align with your highest spiritual potential, it is helpful to start your session with a prayer of your intention. You can adapt the following prayer and change some of the words to be more suitable to your goal if you choose, but keep the same spirit of invoking assistance from above:

> *May I align with my Higher Self's calling today and rise above all that is petty and distracting. May I not take this day for granted, and realize the spirit behind all that is put before me. Great Spirit, fill me with your energy so that I may greater serve others. May I be filled with your compassionate grace so that I may be more patient and understanding with others.*
>
> *Great Spirit, thank you for this day and the aliveness you have given me to experience the beauty and the wonders this day will bring. Thank you for your blessings, and may the good that comes from the gifts you have given me have a ripple effect to improve the lives of others.*

After you have said your prayer of invocation for spiritual assistance, sit in open receptivity and listen for direction. It can be said that prayer is asking something of God and meditating is listening for the answer.

Peak Performance Visualization

Athletes have long known the value of performance visualization before competition to help them prepare, and numerous studies support this practice of mental rehearsal. In his book *Evolve Your Brain,* Joe Dispenza cites a study showing how powerfully mental rehearsal acts on the neural circuitry of the brain itself.

A group of volunteers participated in a five-day study of learning to play a simple piano passage to measure changes taking place in the brain. The first group was taught a specific one-handed, five-finger sequence to play on the piano that they were to practice for two hours a day over the course of the five-day study. The second group was just encouraged to play whatever notes they wanted to, without any instruction. The third group observed and watched the first group play the sequence until they memorized it, and then they were to spend the same two hours a day mentally playing the piece in

After you have said your prayer of
invocation for spiritual assistance,
sit in open receptivity and
listen for direction. It can be said
that prayer is asking something
of God and meditating is
listening for the answer.

their mind. A fourth group was the control group and did nothing at all.

The scientists conducting the experiment used a sensitive cranial magnetic stimulation device to measure changes in the circuitry of the participants' brains during the testing period. The group that just watched and then visualized playing the piece with mental rehearsal showed almost the same changes in neural circuitry in the same areas of the brain as the first group that actually played the piano, while the second group playing randomly showed little change and the control group showed none.

Studies like these and many others support the finding that meditators learn to train their minds: firing is wiring in consciousness. The neural networks activated in your brain while visualizing an activity with mental rehearsal are the same ones that are activated when you are actually doing the activity. The applications for utilizing this technique to bring out peak performance are endless. Whether it be an athletic event, a performance of any type, an important responsibility you have to rise up and meet, an important meeting you want to be at your best for, or countless other activities, spending time in pre-performance visualization of you doing exactly what you need to do will definitely help pave the way to your success.

For mental rehearsal to be effective, it must be as methodical and focused as if performing the actual experience. Structure your mental rehearsal the same as if you were actually practicing by evaluating your progress and making necessary corrections to sharpen your inner practice.

Guidance on Worldly Dilemmas

When you have been grappling with a worldly dilemma for an extended period of time and still have not determined the right course of action to take, try turning your problem over to your Higher Self for guidance. Let's say you have a disruptive employee who does good work but has a difficult time getting along with other employees, and you are trying to decide whether to give the person further guidance or a termination notice. First contemplate your dilemma at the beginning stage of your meditation, then turn it over to your Higher Self and surrender into the meditative state and no longer think about the issue at hand. After resting in the tranquility of your Higher Self for a time, reconsider your dilemma and know the truth from your Higher Self. Then act on it.

Transmuting Negative Energy

When you are experiencing negative energy, like being mad, angry, or frustrated, you experience a great deal of energy. The trouble is, it is negative energy. Energy is energy and can be transformed from negative to positive energy, but first it has to be owned. When you say *I am angry* or *I am mad*, you can feel the powerful energy build. As soon as you put a label on the reason you are mad, you give away your power to whatever you say is the reason you are upset. If you own the energy, you can work with it.

First look at the current situation as a screen that you are projecting your energy onto. Tell yourself that if it was not this current situation that was making you mad or frustrated, then it would be a hundred others. Let go of the event as the important issue and work with the energy of the moment itself. Instead of being mad at _____, just be mad. Instead of being frustrated because of _____, just be frustrated.

Now imagine that you are breathing all of this hot, negative energy into your body, and picture it as a seething, dark ball low in your spine.

Let go of the image of the dark ball of energy and turn your attention to your heart, and picture it as a fiery orb of energy. Breathe a couple of deep breaths into your heart and picture the flames dancing brightly.

Now go back to the image of the dark ball deep in your spine, and breathe deep into it. On the inbreath, coax the dark ball of energy up your spine in your mind's eye, and when it reaches your heart, picture all of the darkness being burned away, leaving clear, radiant energy. Feel this energy filling your body, and now that it has been liberated, you are free to work with it in any way you choose.

• EXERCISE 24 •
Breaking Free from Needless Worry

This exercise was inspired by the spiritual teacher and author Byron Katie and her techniques for liberating ourselves from false beliefs and concerns that limit our ability to live fully and freely. I had been watching a video of hers explaining her process, when later in the day a crown broke off one of my teeth while eating lunch. Although it wasn't painful, it looked terrible and I was going out of town in a few days for a speaking engagement, so I was quite anxious to get it taken care of immediately. I called my dentist and left a message, and waited for a call back.

While waiting, I began to worry about all the possible outcomes: *What if the dentist can't see me before I have to leave? What if I have to cancel my trip because of this? What if she can see me but it will cost a ton because it is an emergency visit?* Not having dental insurance, I imagined this was going to be a huge hit on my finances. All of these considerations felt terrible.

Then I recalled the teaching I had listened to that very morning about how energetically draining it is to worry about things we don't even know are true and how to break free from this annoying tendency. I practiced an abbreviated version of this exercise and stayed open to the mystery of how the situation would unfold, rather than feeling anxious about possible outcomes. The following is the simplified method I have adopted.

First sit in a comfortable position in a quiet place that supports your time for inner contemplation. Take several deep, relaxing breaths to center yourself. Now let your breath return to its normal rhythm and follow the subtle rising and falling of your energy field with each inbreath and outbreath. Pay particular attention to the moment when your breath changes from one phase to the other, and notice the little gap in between. After several minutes of bringing your attention back to your breath, the mental chatter begins to quiet down, and you become aware that you are aware of the mental dialogue going on within your still awareness.

This is a necessary first step in all investigations of awareness based on self-inquiry. First awaken to awareness, then investigate with self-inquiry.

Asking yourself the following two questions can be effective in dealing with all types of anxiety, fear, and worry. First ask yourself *How does this worry make me feel energetically as I consider its possibilities?* And secondly ask yourself *Is it absolutely true and certain that this situation will turn out poorly for me?*

If I cannot be certain that something I am worried or concerned about is even the truth, I have learned to drop the needless worry, particularly when it makes me feel terrible. There are so many things that are valuable to spend time thinking about, so why waste time and deplete your energy by ruminating on things that you don't even know are based in truth?

After doing this exercise, I realized that I really didn't know the truth of how the situation with my tooth was going to play out, so I did my best to just stay open to the mystery of what was going to happen and I went back to preparing for my upcoming trip. Not long after that, I received a call from the dentist confirming that she could squeeze me in the next day due to my dire circumstances. I was at least thankful for that, and went to the appointment as receptive to the assistance as I could be.

As I sat down in the dentist's chair, she was expressing her frustration at having to battle with insurance companies for payment. As she began the work, she completed her venting by saying that it just wasn't right that the insurance companies were driving the prices up and challenging payments. She felt that people like me who paid cash for their dental work were being treated unfairly by these increasing prices, and she said she just felt like doing something about it. It was a fairly long and somewhat complicated procedure, and when we were finished and I went to the cashier, I was told that since I was paying cash, the dentist wanted to charge me only a hundred dollars for the work!

I was more than thankful for how fortunate I was to have things work out this way and how much time I might have wasted in needless worry had I not done the exercise of examining the truth of what I was considering. I know my mind well enough to see that there have been many times when I have wasted time and energy worrying about issues that never manifested at all. By practicing this simple exercise of examining the truth of my concerns, I am learning to break free from this tendency and focus my mind on useful activities such as research and writing, which I thoroughly enjoy.

For those of you who have or work with children, the following chapter provides many tips and exercises for introducing meditation to children so they may start receiving the benefits of this inner discipline at an early age.

Chapter Six

MEDITATION
FOR CHILDREN

Meditation training for young children can be very beneficial, particularly in our modern world with so many distractions pulling at their attention. Learning to calm their busy minds and train their attention to go where they want it to go will benefit their concentration ability in all aspects of learning. Beginning mindfulness exercises helps children learn how to relax, let go of stress, and connect with their own inner source of calm.

Practices for focusing their attention help them develop an improved attention span, leading to less hyperactivity.

Early mindfulness training leads to a better sense of self-esteem and improves family relationships. Social anxiety diminishes, and friendships and social life are greatly enhanced. Many studies (including "Mindfulness Meditation Training in Adults and Adolescents with ADHD" by a group of researchers led by Lidia Zylowska in 2008) have shown that with mindfulness training, children with attention deficit disorder have an improved attention span and often need less medication to control their symptoms.

Mindfulness training for teenagers in learning to sit and watch their thoughts and emotions rise and fall without reacting, just watching, is an excellent practice for the often emotionally tumultuous teenage years. Youths who have mindfulness training are not nearly as vulnerable to the emotional storms that often come from early social encounters. They have developed the ability to watch the comings and goings of their thoughts and emotions and have become more adept at not reacting to these tugs and pulls and staying in centered awareness.

Another factor contributing to the improved self-confidence of young meditators is that the training of mindfulness diminishes the "me" center and its impact on the flow of interactions throughout the day, freeing them from the anxiety of taking everything so personally. In the teenage years, when the development of a personal identity is so important, taking everything personally and overreacting to even the hint of a slight from others often comes with the territory. With mindfulness training, this defensive reaction diminishes as practitioners develop greater skill at remaining unruffled by whatever happens in life.

Imagine the benefit for teenagers to know that every thought and emotion that arises in them throughout the day does not mean something is wrong with them! It is one thing to learn not to take everything that others say about you personally, but learning how to not take their own thoughts and emotions so personally gives teens a greater ability to stay unruffled in the face of trying situations.

Very young children can work with mindfulness training, focused attention, breath awareness, and all types of visualization exercises to help them train their minds. Of course they will need your assistance and participation, and this can be a wonderful quiet-time activity to take part in together. In the following exercises, instructions for you are given first, and then, where the quotation marks begin, are the passages to read to your child.

To avoid the awkwardness of writing "his or her" each time in referring to your child, genders will be alternated with each exercise.

Breath Awareness for Children

Teaching children breathing exercises is an excellent starting point for mindfulness training. There is nothing more immediate than our next breath, and training children to follow their breath is the surest way to help them come back to the here and now.

• EXERCISE 26 •
Hands on Belly

Have your child sit cross-legged on the floor or a chair, with hands resting palms up on her thighs. Then offer the following direction:

"Sit as if you were a mountain, with your spine straight and tall. Relax your shoulders, relax your mouth and eyes, and be as still and quiet as a mountain. Now place your hands on your belly and take a deep breath into your belly and feel that it is rising and expanding, and as you breathe out, feel your belly falling and flattening. Let your breath be natural, and feel the rising and flattening of your belly with your breath. As your belly rises, say *rising* silently to yourself, and as your belly falls on the outbreath, say *falling* silently to yourself. Do this for two minutes.

"Now return to your normal breathing and notice how your body feels."

• EXERCISE 27 •
Ocean Breath

Children enjoy this exercise and often find the sound of their ocean breath quite relaxing. First have your child sit with his hands on his lap with palms up, spine straight and tall, being as quiet and still as a mountain. Direct your child to relax his shoulders, face, and entire body. Direct his attention to his breath, and encourage him to follow it down to his belly and back up through the nose.

Now have your child hold his lips in a loose *O* while slightly tightening the back of the throat, so that both the inbreath and the outbreath sound like ocean waves. Have your child practice ocean breath for two minutes and then return to natural breathing. Now direct your child to stop and feel the effects of this exercise on his body and mind.

Next, close your right nostril
and open your left nostril as
you breathe out on the left side.
To complete one cycle,
keep your left nostril open
as you breathe in on the left side.
Have your child repeat this cycle
for two minutes. Then have her
place both hands on her legs
and just breathe normally
and notice how she feels
after this exercise.

Alternate Nostril Breathing

This exercise is excellent for children to bring balance to their energy field. You can offer these directions:

"First sit with your spine straight and tall and place your left hand on your left leg with your palm up. Lift your right hand to your nose and place your thumb gently on your right nostril and your ring finger [you might need to identify the ring finger] gently on your left nostril. Place your middle and index fingers lightly on your brow. Now gently close your right nostril with your thumb and breathe in through your open left nostril.

"Next, close your left nostril with your ring finger and open your right nostril as you breathe out. Then keep your left nostril closed and your right nostril open as you breathe in on the right side.

"Next, close your right nostril and open your left nostril as you breathe out on the left side.

"To complete one cycle, keep your left nostril open as you breathe in on the left side."

Have your child repeat this cycle for two minutes. Then have her place both hands on her legs and just breathe normally and notice how she feels after this exercise.

Breath and Body Awareness

This exercise is suitable for people of all ages and is particularly helpful to introduce children to meditation.

First have your child sit in a comfortable position, with a straight spine, the head and ears in alignment with the spine, and the head tilted slightly forward. This can be in a chair, with the feet flat on the floor and hands palms down resting on the thighs (palms down to direct sensitivity to the body). If your child is able to sit cross-legged or in lotus posture on the floor, all the better, as children are typically able to do this with more ease than adults, and they often enjoy being able to sit in postures that adults have difficulty with. Offer these instructions:

"Now with your eyes closed, focus on your breath. Let your breath become even and steady, breathing all the way to your belly and then gently exhaling naturally. Place your hands on your belly and feel it getting bigger with your inbreath and getting smaller with your out-breath. Do this for ten rounds, counting on each exhale.

"Now tell yourself that you would like to have your whole body relax. Notice wherever your body doesn't feel soft and relaxed, and imagine in your mind's eye that you are sending a beam of warm light to the tight area, making it soft and relaxed. Breathe right into the tight area, projecting your beam of light with your breath. Go wherever you first notice any tight feelings, most often the neck and shoulders, and breathe into the tension until it dissolves. Relax your eyes and face muscles and then move your beam of light throughout your body, noticing any tight feelings in your stomach, chest, or heart. Breathe into the tension and dissolve it.

"Now stop and feel the effects. Sit with this relaxed feeling of well-being as long as you like."

When I was first learning yoga, my teacher would have us do a series of exercises and then lie down in corpse pose with this directive: "Now stop and feel the effects." We would just lie there, taking note of how our bodies felt and noticing any subtle differences from our practice. I find this to be great advice for your child to periodically stop and feel the effects of whatever practice you are teaching. This cultivates mindfulness and awareness of sensations arising within the body and mind.

• EXERCISE 30 •

Loving-Kindness Training for Children

This type of meditation is particularly accessible for children and can be easily taught. This practice has a long-term transforming effect on the psyche and improves children's social skills by awakening in them a compassionate interest in the well-being of others.

Children are particularly adept at imagination and visualization exercises. For children, loving-kindness practice is much the same as it is with adults, but you change the phrases and images to make them age-appropriate. Offer these instructions:

"First sit tall in your chair. Feel your feet touch the ground and your hands resting on your legs. Notice your breath in its natural rhythm without any effort on your part. Follow your inbreath from your nose down through your lungs and into your belly. Now follow your outbreath from your belly up through your nose. Do this a few times and pay attention to the moment your breath changes from the inbreath to the outbreath and from the outbreath to the inbreath.

"Now you are going to send friendly thoughts to someone you care about. You could picture a friend, someone in your family, or a favorite pet that you would like to send your friendly thoughts to. Hold on to your friend's image and silently say the following in your mind:

I wish for you to be happy.
I wish for you to be free of all bad feelings.
I wish for you to be safe and loved by others.
I wish for you to be filled with love and kindness.

"Say these friendly wishes several times, picturing that you are sending the energy of these phrases to your friend's heart. With each time you send your friendly wishes to your friend, picture energy filling your friend with light and warmth.

"After you have done this for a few minutes, see your friend sending you these same friendly thoughts directed to your heart. Imagine your friend saying the following to you:

I wish for you to be happy.
I wish for you to be free of all bad feelings.
I wish for you to feel safe and loved by others.
I wish for you to be filled with love and kindness.

"Imagine hearing your friend's words several times, and with each time, the energy in your heart grows and grows to ultimately fill your entire being with its light and warmth. Rest in this feeling and notice how you feel after this exercise."

After the children have learned this, they can then extend their circle of loving-kindness to include their family, all of the children at school (even ones they have had difficulties with), the whole community, and ultimately the whole world and all of its creatures.

Visualizations for Bedtime

An excellent time to have children practice visualization exercises to help them quiet their minds is while you are helping them get ready for bed and are tucking them in for the night. There are fewer distractions calling for their attention, and the visualizations help them go to sleep peacefully.

• EXERCISE 31 •

The Inner Smile

This visualization exercise is excellent for children and is particularly helpful before bedtime to help them enter the dreamtime with a warm, loving, secure feeling within. Providing children with this training can be an excellent resource for them when they are confronted with troubling dreams or thoughts. They can do this practice to restore a sense of inner happiness.

This exercise can be done while sitting in the daytime or when lying down at bedtime. First have your child close her eyes and imagine a friend, a loved one, or a favorite pet in her mind's eye, and let the feeling of a smile come over her face. Have her visualize the energy of the smile coming through her eyes as if she were smiling through her eyes.

Tell her to take this energy of the smile on a journey through her entire body. Have her focus the energy beam of her smile on the inside of her head and brain. Encourage her to smile through her throat and then her chest and lungs, and then let the energy of the smile settle into her heart. Ask her to enjoy a few breaths from her smiling heart, and then take her smile into her stomach, lower abdomen, and all the way to the base of the spine. Have her imagine every cell in her body smiling and happy, as if her entire body were radiating a smile. Now have her stop and feel the effects of this practice while basking in this healing radiance.

• EXERCISE 32 •

Redirecting Fear

Very young children are not ready for meditation training in the formal sense, but teaching them to steady their minds with a focus on their breathing and then guiding them into visualizations can be very helpful before going to sleep. It can be terrifying for young children to be alone in the dark with just their imagination. Parents often seek to alleviate young children's fears with a statement such as "Don't worry about that—it's just your imagination." This identifies the problem, but the child is still stuck with their imagination, which can't just simply be dismissed as if it isn't real. Although imagination is not tangible, the experience of their imagination trapped in a fearful place is very real and scary indeed.

As an alternative to dismissing our children's imagination, we could again identify the source of their fears as imagination and then teach them how to use their imagination in empowering ways, as in the following example:

"That is your imagination and it can get scary, right? Do you know that you can train your imagination to be your friend and help you feel good?

"First snuggle into a comfy position. Now just follow your breath with your attention. Notice it on your inbreath as it goes down to your belly and how your belly gets bigger, then notice how your belly gently flattens on the outbreath. Can you do this five times?

"Now let's go to your imagination, and imagine the sky above you filled with twinkling stars and a bright full moon. These are the nighttime lights. Notice how their lights are soft and soothing. Different from the sun's light in the daytime, these gentle lights are your nighttime friends.

"Now imagine that you can gather these twinkling, soft lights into your forehead. Can you see the lights twinkling in your mind's eye? Now imagine that you can breathe these inner lights all the way down to your belly, and with each breath, these nighttime lights are spreading throughout your whole body. How do you feel as you imagine these starlights twinkling throughout your body as you go to sleep?"

In the concluding chapter, we will further explore incorporating the benefits of meditation into everyday life.

Conclusion

MINDFULNESS IN DAILY LIFE

We have explored many different styles and applications of meditation throughout this book, and as you have learned, meditation is not simply sitting and doing nothing—it is actively training your mind to quiet so you can focus on your spiritual essence. It is training your mind to enter into a listening mode of being and awakening into awareness. The awareness you awaken to in meditation can be carried over into daily life by practicing mindfulness throughout the day—staying in open, receptive awareness of whatever is arising in the mind and body, moment by moment, throughout the day.

Mindfulness comes from the Pali word *sati,* meaning awareness or non-forgetfulness. With mindfulness practice throughout the day, you are not trying to avoid anxiety, sadness, fear, or any other undesired mental state; you are learning to accept whatever arises, with moment-to-moment awareness of the sensations of the body and the thoughts associated with the sensations, with an open, investigative attitude.

There are three components of practicing mindfulness. First, stay in the present moment. Second, cultivate the ability to observe yourself in action by staying consciously aware of the thoughts moving through your mind and the sensations arising in your body from moment to moment. Third, cultivate an open, receptive, and even loving attitude toward whatever is arising.

The third stage of cultivating an open, receptive, loving attitude is what melts away the fortress of old ways of being. Without this open acceptance, you can be observing yourself maintaining old patterns with a judgmental attitude, locking you into a battle with yourself and allowing the old patterns to persist. With loving acceptance, frozen patterns begin to melt and dissolve.

Instead of working on avoiding any mental state, you are expanding your capacity to tolerate all mental states, including discomfort, and even to bear adversity. With mindfulness, you are cultivating ease in your psyche, but not by avoiding anxiety or fear when they arise. In a sense, you lean into these undesirable feelings with an investigative awareness and discover that they will dissipate, much like an early morning fog burns off as the sun warms it. In yoga, we learn to breathe into the sensations/pain of the stretch—accept it—know what it is—and then on the outbreath, we relax the muscles further and deepen the stretch. Mindfulness is like this: Accept whatever sensations are arising in your body and emotions and breathe into them, then on an outbreath, relax further into accepting the sensations just as they are.

As you first begin to practice mindfulness throughout the day, you may be shocked to discover just how often you slip into mindlessness—engaging the mind's tendency to dwell on the past or anticipate the future. You might discover that the vast majority of your day is spent lost in thought streams of either avoidance or grasping—trying to avoid something unpleasant or thinking of something more desirable than this moment. Each time you become aware that you are lost in your thoughts, gently pull your attention back to your breath and the sensations arising in your body. Focusing on your breath and body serves as an anchor, a touch-base for the mind, rooted in the present moment.

Be patient and gentle with yourself in your efforts to stay mindful throughout the day. Training your mind to stay in the present is like training a puppy to sit and stay on command. It takes patience and loving acceptance to teach the puppy, and this is also the best way to approach training your unruly mind to stay present.

One thing we all learn in life is that we have very little control of others and how they act. There is so much of life that you cannot control, with your share of joys and sorrows, losses and gains, successes and failures. However, with mindfulness practice, you learn to take control of the one thing you do have power over: how you react and respond to life. Your happiness and peace of mind are conditions within you and your mind, and therefore the causes for this inner well-being cannot be found outside of your mind. With mindfulness practice, you learn to break free of the tendency to look to others and conditions in the world as the causes of either your happiness or your unhappiness—you train yourself to work with these issues at their source within you.

With mindfulness practice, you learn
to take control of the one thing you
do have power over: how you react and
respond to life. Your happiness and
peace of mind are conditions within you
and your mind, and therefore the causes
for this inner well-being cannot be found
outside of your mind. With mindfulness
practice, you learn to break free of
the tendency to look to others and
conditions in the world as the causes
of either your happiness or your
unhappiness—you train yourself to
work with these issues at
their source within you.

There is a story about a teacher in times gone by who was traveling from village to village to share his knowledge of finding inner peace. It happened that in one village he visited, he attracted an unfriendly audience. As he began to tell his story, members of the audience taunted and jeered at him, seeking more lively entertainment. They continued their rude behavior while he calmly waited. After noticing his unruffled demeanor in the face of their taunting, one person in the crowd spoke up: "How is it that you do not seem to be bothered by us, while we clearly don't like what you are saying?"

The teacher responded, "How you choose to act is up to you, and how I respond is up to me. Why would I let your choosing to be rude disturb my peace of mind?"

And this is what you learn through practicing mindfulness. You are able to be like the teacher in the story when your mind wants to react in a negative way to something or other, and you are able to observe this without getting pulled into the story.

Observing your mind and body's reactions to life, in and of itself, changes your experience. However, simply watching and observing yourself is not enough to be considered mindfulness. You must also cultivate an open and accepting attitude. You could be observing yourself with a negative, critical eye. What you pay attention to grows, and without being mindful of your attitude, you could be fueling your negativity. Cultivating the attitude of staying mindful with an open and loving acceptance of whatever is arising will train the mind to stay at ease and free of reactions.

Mindfulness is not simply a passive approach to life—you will still have your goals, your drive to achieve, and your passions; but mindfulness does allow your true self to shine through so that your goals and passions are aligned with your true nature. Mindfulness allows you to be discerning about which thoughts and emotions to act on and which ones to pass on, allowing you to become more focused in all of your endeavors.

Another long-term benefit of mindfulness in daily life is how much easier it becomes to shed unwanted habits that were previously used to escape the moment. With your practice of staying consciously aware in open acceptance of this moment, you have seen through the illusion of attempting to escape this moment, this "now," to find a better now. You have learned that there is nothing to escape from, and unwanted habits and previous means of distracting yourself can be shed with very little effort.

Mindfulness practice is staying aware of the thoughts and sensations arising in your body from moment to moment, just as is practiced in Vipassana meditation (discussed in chapter 4). The connection between sensations arising in your body and the thoughts moving through your mind becomes a valuable monitor throughout the day. As you stay aware of sensations arising in the body and the attendant thoughts that are simultaneously occurring, you learn just how much your thoughts, feelings, and emotions are interconnected within you. When you feel a strong sensation or emotion arising in your body, take note of what you are thinking about in the very moment you notice the sensation. You will see specifically how certain thought streams stir particular sensations and emotional feelings, as well as the inverse: how certain sensations stir particular thought streams.

A sudden rush of anxiety is a familiar example of this connection. You can be going along with your day and all is well, when suddenly anxious feelings of inadequacy wash over you. Your pulse quickens and your breath is shallow, constricted, or held tight—your amygdala is pumping fight-or-flight hormones into your system and you feel like you want to jump out of your skin.

In this example of a strong sensation disrupting your ease of being, train yourself to notice specifically what you are thinking about exactly when you notice the sensations of anxiety. Pay attention to when you notice the thought stream associated with the sensations: Are you becoming aware of it at the beginning of the thought, in the middle of it, or after it has passed? Pay attention to specific sensations occurring within your body, your skin, and your breath.

By staying attentive to this connection between what you are thinking about and how you are feeling, you see how your mental processes have created much of the difficulty you have experienced in life. Knowing your mental patterns is the first step to altering those patterns, followed by training yourself to move away from thought streams that pull you out of a sense of ease.

Mindfulness training throughout the day helps you maintain a sense of ease in two ways. First, it expands your range of what is tolerable, allowing you to stay with experiences without needing to change what is going on. Second, by noticing what you are thinking about when sensations, feelings, and emotions arise in your body, you are able to name what you are experiencing, such as *anxious feelings*, *memory*, or *anticipation*, allowing you to essentially stand outside of the experience—if you can name "it," you are not "it."

You can sharpen your skill at recognizing these connections by training yourself to catch reactionary thoughts as soon as possible in the process, allowing you to make adjustments ultimately even before a disturbance in your mind begins.

There is a teaching in Buddhism referred to as the *Eight Vicissitudes* that everyone will experience cyclically throughout their life: loss and gain, disrespect and fame, praise and blame, pleasure and pain. Each of these is an impermanent, temporary state.

All of us have had these experiences: some losses and some gains, times of recognition and times when our character is questioned, times of being praised and times of being blamed, times of great pleasure as well as times of pain.

The teaching behind the Eight Vicissitudes is that the wise person knows that attaching oneself to preferred states and avoiding the undesired states is futile—all is changing in cyclic measure. By cultivating mindfulness, you learn to abide in the place within you that is aware of these changing cycles, resting peacefully within, observing but not attaching yourself to the highs and lows of this human existence.

It is important to maintain a regular meditation practice of your choice to sustain the benefits; otherwise, it is very easy for the mind to slip back into its old ways. With regular practice, your clarity improves, enhancing your ability to see things as they actually are—without judgment. Defensiveness toward others transforms into empathy and curiosity about their experiences. By practicing regularly, you create new neural networks in your brain—neurons that fire together create new patterns of responding to others, making it easier and easier to sustain a state of calm awareness inside while engaging in life outwardly.

If you continue your meditation practice for the rest of your life, you will do much to preserve your brain and slow down its natural aging process. Gray matter is the tissue holding the neurons and circuitry of the brain, allowing the brain to communicate with all parts of itself. Although there is a natural loss of gray matter in the brain caused by aging, studies (such as the one by a group of researchers at UCLA led by Eileen Luders in 2014) show that those who have meditated for twenty years show significantly less loss of gray matter throughout their entire brains compared to those of the same age group who did not practice this inner discipline.

Changing the Inner Dialogue from Chatter to Higher-Mind Coaching

Even after years of training in quieting your mind, the inner voices remain. However, you can change the source of your inner dialogue so that you are not listening to the chatter of your Lower Self—instead, you can rewire your mental circuitry to listen to the direction and prompt-ings of your Higher Self. Sometimes called the still, quiet voice within, it is there, but it is often drowned out by the busy traffic of the everyday mind.

Your Higher Self can be your guide that is with you all day long—coaching you, encouraging you, and remind-ing you when you drift out of awareness. Train yourself to listen to that voice. *If there is going to be an inner dialogue going on all day long anyway, let it be with your Higher Self.*

When you are dealing with a difficult emotion, let your Higher Self encourage and coach your Lower Self back to a state of ease of mind. Tell yourself *It's okay, we can handle this. This too shall pass, and I can accept this.* This is training yourself to move away from aversion. Aversion is just as strong as desire in skewing your perception of the truth of the moment. With aversion comes a tightening of your energy field, narrowing your range of what you can experience in life. By attempting to control life to fit in

conclusion

198

with what is acceptable to you, this narrowing of what is tolerable limits the highs as well.

As you continue with your meditation practice, your energy field begins to change and have a subtle influence on those you come in contact with. Even if only one person in a family is meditating, the whole family benefits from there being a peaceful center in the midst of all the family chaos. Even if only one person in a relationship is meditating, the relationship is benefitted by the increased openness and diminished defensiveness of the meditator. Even if only one person in a workplace is meditating, the entire workplace benefits from the peaceful, calm presence of the one.

Whatever your lifestyle, know that as a meditator you are becoming a demonstration of how to live in peace and ease with yourself in a world that is often troubled. *With the changes that take place within you, you are in the same world as others but not of the same world.* You are being sustained from a different source. Know that your efforts will have a ripple effect, supporting others seeking to soothe their troubled minds.

May you find inner peace and fulfillment from your meditation practice, and may you share your glad heart and peaceful presence with others in the world.

BIBLIOGRAPHY

Adyashanti. *Falling into Grace*. Boulder, CO: Sounds True, 2011.

——. *True Meditation*. Boulder, CO: Sounds True, 2006.

Bancroft, Anne, ed. *The Dhammapada*. Rockport, MA: Element, 1997.

Barks, Coleman, trans. *The Essential Rumi*. San Francisco, CA: Harper, 1995.

Chödrön, Pema. *When Things Fall Apart*. Boston, MA: Shambhala, 1997.

Dispenza, Joe. *Evolve Your Brain: The Science of Changing Your Mind*. Deerfield Beach, FL: Health Communications, Inc., 2007.

Doty, James R. *Into the Magic Shop*. New York: Avery, 2016.

Easwaran, Eknath, trans. *The Bhagavad Gita*. Tomales, CA: Nilgiri Press, 1985.

———. *Meditation: A Simple Eight-Point Program for Translating Spiritual Ideals into Daily Life.* Tomales, CA: Nilgiri Press, 1978.

Goldstein, Joseph, and Jack Kornfield. *Seeking the Heart of Wisdom: The Path of Insight Meditation.* Boston, MA: Shambhala, 1987.

Long, Max Freedom. *The Secret Science at Work.* Los Angeles, CA: Huna Research Publications, 1953.

Luders, Eileen, et al. "Forever Young(er): Potential Age-Defying Effects of Long-Term Meditation on Gray Matter Atrophy." *Frontiers in Psychology* 5 (2014): 1551.

Mitchell, Stephen, ed. *Tao Te Ching.* New York: Harper & Row, 1991.

Nhat Hanh, Thich. *Being Peace.* Berkeley, CA: Parallax Press, 1987.

———. *Peace Is Every Step.* New York: Bantam Books, 1991.

Nisargadatta, Maharaj. *I Am That.* 1973. Reprint, Durham, NC: The Acorn Press, 1982.

Osborne, Arthur, ed. *The Teachings of Ramana Maharshi.* 1962. Reprint, York Beach, ME: Samuel Weiser, 1996.

Pond, David. *Chakras Beyond Beginners.* Woodbury, MN: Llewellyn, 2016.

———. *Chakras for Beginners.* St. Paul, MN: Llewellyn, 1999.

———. *The Pursuit of Happiness.* Woodbury, MN: Llewellyn, 2008.

———. *Western Seeker, Eastern Paths.* St. Paul, MN: Llewellyn, 2003.

Radin, Dean. *Supernormal: Science, Yoga, and the Evidence for Extraordinary Psychic Abilities.* New York: Deepak Chopra Books, 2013.

Reps, Paul, comp. *Zen Flesh, Zen Bones.* Tokyo, Rutland, VT: C. E. Tuttle Co., 1957.

Ricard, Matthieu. *Happiness: A Guide to Developing Life's Most Important Skill.* Paris: NiL Editions, 2003.

Rinpoche, Sogyal. *The Tibetan Book of Living and Dying.* San Francisco, CA: Harper, 1992.

Salzberg, Sharon. *Lovingkindness.* Boston, MA: Shambhala, 1997.

Shearer, Alistair, trans. and intro. *The Yoga Sutras of Patanjali.* New York: Bell Tower, 1982.

Tolle, Eckhart. *The Power of Now*. Vancouver, Canada: Namaste Publishing, 2004.

Whitman, Walt. *Leaves of Grass*. Brooklyn, NY: Self-published, 1855.

Yogananda, Paramahansa. *The Art of Super Realization*. Los Angeles, CA: Yogoda Satsanga Society, 1930.

———. *The Autobiography of a Yogi*. Los Angeles, CA: Self-Realization Fellowship, 1956.

Zylowska, Lidia, et al. "Mindfulness Meditation Training in Adults and Adolescents with ADHD." *Journal of Attention Disorders* 11, no. 6 (May 2008): 737–46.